RECKLESS
WALTER RHEIN
TRAVELER

Tales From a Decade
Abroad

Perseid Press
P. O. Box 584
Centerville, MA 02632

Book design by Sarah Hulcy; cover design by Walter Rhein
Cover image copyright © Perseid Press, 2013.
Cover art Walter Rhein

Trade: ISBN-10: 0991465482, ISBN-13: 978-0-9914654-8-4
ePub: ISBN-10 0986414069, ISBN-13 978-0-9864140-6-0
Kindle: ISBN-10 0986414077, ISBN-13 978-0-9864140-7-7
Published in the United States of America

10 9 8 7 6 5 4 3 2 1

Acknowledgements

I received help from a wonderful community of people on this book. I'd like to thank Doug Berg, Mary Flood, Mike Gasparovic, Sarah Hulcy, Chris Morris, Janet Morris, and Cas Peace for their insight, contributions, and hard work. Also, thanks to all the friends and fellow travelers I've met along the way.

Reckless

Traveler

Dedication

For

S. A. Z.

Table of Contents

Reckless

Traveler

Chapter 1

Kidnapped by Terrorists

The motor coach slammed to a halt, waking me and every other passenger who had purchased a ticket from Lima to Guayaquil. The thirty hour trip should have been nearing its end, but some inner sense immune to the grogginess of slumber evoked a tingle of concern about this unscheduled stop. I rubbed my eyes and peered through the grimy portal only to be jolted sober at the sight of a group of armed men emerging from the depths of the Ecuadorian foliage.

Perhaps twenty soldiers approached our hapless vehicle which lounged motionless, fat and pitiful in the muddy ruts of an obscure provincial highway. The riflemen spread out to surround the vehicle in the same fashion that a pack of wolves approaches the carcass of a newly fallen kill. Most of the men wore some sort of camouflage, but not the precise, orderly camouflage common to the official military force of a sovereign nation.

No. This unit had been clad piecemeal, perhaps by stripping away bloodstained scraps from countless cadavers littered on forgotten battlefields which no government would ever acknowledge. Their grim economy of movement telegraphed the harsh, soul-wrenching depression of warfare.

These weren't soldiers, they were mercenaries — or worse.

Some of the men had beards, some not; some had bright red bandanas tied around their heads; some smoked. All displayed the wary weariness of hungry predators.

They all carried AK-47s. I wasn't the best military expert in the world, but I'd seen all the *Rambo* films, and I could recognize an AK-47, the weapon that Rambo stripped from some fallen opponent — the weapon he used whenever all other options failed. To anyone born in the United States, the AK-47 was symbolically loaded: the weapon of the enemy.

All at once, every nagging subconscious voice that ever called me a fool for choosing to live in South America jeered at me in chorus:

"What are you thinking?"

"You're going to get yourself killed!"

"Why can't you live someplace safe?"

I'd always considered the danger of South America exaggerated, a cultivated lie meant to justify the repression of a restless populace. Today, from my seat in the small charter bus, it looked as though those voices would have the last laugh.

The troops began marking off a wide perimeter. They were making a big show of this task, as if they had a checklist which they weren't in any rush to complete. Their maneuvers were pure posturing, of course: designed only to demonstrate who was in charge.

The other passengers and I could only watch and do nothing.

I sighed and reached for my pill bottle.

Outside, a dozen mercenaries kicked the tires while two more stood back, nodding, and others dug through the luggage compartment.

One glanced up at the line of glass windows, and everyone who had been watching the proceedings dutifully averted their eyes.

For the first time, I noticed that everyone on the bus was silent. There was a palpable tension in the air. Most of the people on the bus were bronze-skinned travelers, local folk of simple means. One or two of the eldest attempted to project a lack of concern, but their casual body language was too forced to be believed. I caught some of the younger ones stealing sorrowful glances at me: I was the only foreigner on the bus.

When traveling abroad, it's disheartening to catch the locals giving you worried looks.

I sighed again and tried to estimate how many motion-sickness pills to take when faced with mercenaries holding AK-47s. I decided on four, twisted open the bottle, and gulped them down.

Thank goodness for modern medication. There are cowards out there who think you should only use those miraculous little pills in moderation, but the creatively inclined can find ways to fit whatever tool is at their disposal into a proactive response to the problem at hand. I sat still and waited for the pills to take effect.

The mercenaries decided to force the door and climb aboard. The smell of their sweat, gunpowder, and oil permeated the aisle.

Again, they moved slowly, strolling through the bus, hardly glancing at the terrified faces of the people around them. Finally, when they'd all taken positions, one of them spoke:

"All you men: get off the bus and assemble outside."

By then my eyelids were getting a bit heavy, but I pushed the drowsy feeling aside and stood up. From the aisle, I reached into the overhead compartment to grab my backpack.

One of the mercenaries jabbed me sharply in the ribs with his Kalashnikov. "You don't need that," he said.

The barrel of an AK jammed into one's ribs produces a unique electric shock that goes up and down the spine. This sensation cannot be duplicated by anything else.

I shrugged and made my way down the aisle, sensing that my South American adventures were about to end.

It didn't really bother me that much: I'd had a good run.

Then again, my indifference might have only been a result of the pills kicking in. I had ample time to reflect on the matter as I made the long walk down the bus's aisle.

Images of my time in South America floated by like whispers in a waking dream.

Chapter 2

$120 a Month for Rent

"Who's this guy?" asked Marisol, looking at me sideways with an air of suspicion that suggested she'd had several lifetimes of bad experiences with disheveled young backpackers such as myself.

We stood in the small garden between the waist-high wall that lined the street and the reinforced wooden door that provided the entryway into Marisol's house. Marisol stood behind the half-open door, leaning against it for support. She was a middle-aged woman of plain but friendly features and the jet black hair that was common to most Peruvians. I could sense kindness in her face, but also a reluctance to put herself in a position of vulnerability.

"This is my friend," Julia replied. Julia was a young doctor from Germany doing her residency in Perú. She was a tall, attractive woman with red-blonde hair who projected a certain air of authority. She spoke flawless English with a very proper sounding English accent. Julia's Spanish was better than mine, so she had taken it upon herself to act as our translator. "He's looking for a room because he can't stand staying at the Casa Roja any longer."

"The Krishna house?" Marisol said with a slight grin.

"All they do is sing," I piped in, feeling it was safe to do so for the first time. "'Krishna, Krishna, Krishna. Hare, hare, hare.' The words are always the same. I wouldn't mind except that they start at five every morning."

Marisol's half smile didn't expand, but it didn't go away either.

Marisol's one-story house was located just off Avenida Ricardo Palma in the Miraflores district of Lima, Perú. The house was small, quaint, painted white, and the waist-high wall out front succeeded as a worthy replacement for the white picket fence a similar house from back home might have boasted. The inviting, homey ambiance of the place was not disrupted by the bars on the windows or the electric fence running across the roof. Both features were common to all the houses on her block in February, 2002.

"I don't normally rent to men," Marisol said, "because of Jocelyn." Marisol explained that Jocelyn was her twelve-year-old daughter.

On hearing of the child, I began to understand Marisol's caution. Suddenly, the fact that we were having such a discussion at all became something of a miracle.

"I won't be offended if you're uncomfortable," I said with a resigned shrug. "It's no small thing to have a stranger living with you, especially when you have a daughter at an impressionable age."

and attractive women. Their clothing stood out, which struck me as strange since I'd never been one to pay attention to fashion. The cut and the colors of their jackets and pants reminded me of retro US styles from the sixties and seventies. Their ensembles were quite basic, and it put me at ease to think the two of them weren't obsessed with the artificial rigors of superficial physical appearance.

The two of them were naturally lovely. Annika had dusty blonde hair, and Ivonne was a brunette. I liked the way their locks bounced about freely far better than the precise cut achieved from sitting in a stylist's chair for untold hours. The two women both possessed wide smiles that flashed with sparkling white teeth, creating the impression that they were eager to laugh and ready to enjoy themselves.

"This is my friend," Julia said, gesturing at me.

"Where are you from?" Annika asked.

"The US," I said, extending my hand.

The too-formal gesture provoked a look of disapproval. "That's very American," she said, and leaned forward to kiss me on the cheek. That's how they say 'hello' in Perú , and even non-Peruvians adopt the custom when living there.

A kiss is a nice greeting. Getting through the day becomes much easier when dotted with kisses from women you meet.

Introductions finished, we approached a taxi. Julia handled our fare negotiations with the driver. I listened with envy as she navigated a whirlwind of unfamiliar sounds and phrases, all the while fighting back the absurd, uncomfortable notion that I was the topic of their conversation. I'd been fighting that feeling a lot. It's a common sensation when you can't understand the local language. When asked to recall my meager Spanish, I was often left stammering and searching for the traces of familiar words, hammering them together in my mind like a blind cobbler. I'd been told again and again that the older you are the more difficult it is to master a foreign language; I sincerely hoped the oft-repeated axiom proved not to be true.

Negotiations finally over, all five of us piled into the taxi.

"What brought you to Perú?" asked Annika, who had revealed that she was from Denmark. She spoke English with an appealing accent I'd never heard before.

I didn't have a good answer.

"A couple months ago I met a girl from Lima on a beach in Seattle."

Annika giggled. "Ah, so you came down chasing love?"

"Not really, I didn't know her that well."

"Are you still seeing her?"

"No."

"But you're still here," she said.

"I feel compelled to stay."

She giggled more, musically.

"Ah, a muse chaser. How long will you stay around?"

I shrugged.

She smiled, and I was encouraged that she seemed more accepting of this lack of a life plan than others I had encountered.

"Maybe you're not so American after all," she said. "What do your people back home think of you being here?"

Therein lay the rub. "They hate it," I said. "Everybody hates it. When I meet American tourists on the street here, taking 'appropriate' two-week vacations, they flash me disapproving stares as they pass by. Back home, my high school chemistry teacher is furious with me; so is the guy who runs the cash register at the grocery store. They all seem to think I'm violating some unwritten code of cultural behavior."

"How do they know you're living in Perú?" Annika asked.

"Maybe their scorn is only in my imagination," I admitted. "But in the US these days, or at least where I lived, there are those who will label you as 'unpatriotic' for even aspiring to learn a foreign language."

Annika nodded: many in the world thought that Americans were only interested in speaking English. There's a joke that's told abroad: If you speak three languages you're trilingual; if you speak two languages you're bilingual; if you speak one language you're an American.

"What brought you here?" I asked.

She sighed and gazed back out the window.

"My cover is three months of volunteer work, but really I think I'm here for the same reason as you. The volunteer position is a story for my parents to tell so that the grocery store clerk and my high school chemistry teacher do not disapprove of me. I can't explain it, but it's compelling to be someplace so *different*," she explained in her Danish-accented English.

I nodded, pleased to hear I wasn't the only one in the throes of a fundamental curiosity.

"I don't understand how you can be expected to develop your own opinion on anything unless you question what you've been taught to think," I said. "Perhaps it's telling that such challenges of 'common knowledge' are discouraged." That flaw was not limited to Americans; worldwide, opinion was adopted without proof and taken for fact on faith.

The taxi pulled off the highway into a small parking lot beside the beach. On the far side of the highway the cliffs of the "Costa Verde" rose straight up into the air. Buildings sprouted from the tops of the cliffs and sunlight sparkled off the ocean-facing windows of expensive apartments. Overhead, paragliders rode the updraft along the coast. We paid the driver and made the short walk over to the stone-covered beach. The four girls pulled out billowy sheets and arranged them, piling rocks at the corners, and sat. Although cold for swimming or swimwear, the beach had other visitors, watching the sea and listening to the rhythmic crash of the waves.

People on the beach went about their business; surfers in neoprene wetsuits caught small waves to the delight of onlookers, adolescents rolled around with hardly a care that they were out in public, and vendors strolled along selling ice cream or drinks.

Chapter 4

Killing the Bed Bugs

I settled into life in Lima.

My lack of language continued to hobble me, confining me to exploring within walking distance of Marisol's house.

Simply talking with people was taxing. My efforts to communicate left me exhausted. I began to lose weight and take long naps to give my mind a chance to recover.

But still, life was good. I was occupied and challenged. The newness all around exhilarated me.

After about a week, when the shine started wearing off, I began noticing something unpleasant about my living arrangements. During the night, I could depend on being awakened by a sensation like insect bites. I'd reach down, scratch, roll over, and go back to sleep.

In the mornings, I'd wake covered with itchy red welts. These were smaller than the welts you might get from a mosquito bite, itchy rather than painful, but they were still a nuisance.

Initially, these welts became part of the adventure, something to endure in exchange for paying $120 a month in rent.

My enthusiasm carried me for a time but, as with any irritation, the day came when I could no longer tolerate it. My tormentors had a name: bed bugs!

My flimsy grasp of Spanish made communication an exercise in guesswork, and Marisol was particularly bad at comprehending any information I attempted to convey. She had an expert, puppy-dog gaze she'd throw at me in response to even the most obvious conversational requests. Attempting to discuss the bed bugs with her was out of the question.

So every night I faced the bugs once more, unable to avoid becoming the main course in their free buffet.

The answer to my bug problem came to me while I shopped at Wong, the local grocery store. I was desperately searching for a jar of peanut butter — an extremely rare item in Perú — when I got lost and stumbled into an aisle containing all sorts of cleaning products and pest toxins. Every grocery store in the world has such an aisle, and it's kind of strange when you think about it: there you are, standing in the major food source for an entire community, yet right beside all the produce is an assortment of lethal poisons in convenient aerosol containers.

I still had peanut butter on the brain when I happened to glance down at a bottle of *Raid*. At first, the purpose of the can didn't register. I continued to quest for peanut butter, but the longer my search went unfulfilled, the more my mind began to wander. The spray can continued to draw my eyes, and suddenly I realized how the *Raid* might solve my bug problem.

I glanced at the welts on my arm. Certainly if the *Raid* could kill wasps, it would have no problem dealing with some pesky bed bugs!

Grabbing a spray bottle of *Raid*, I headed first to the cash register and then toward Marisol's house, buoyed by a new sense of purpose.

Marisol was standing by the door when I got there. I waved at her politely and smuggled the contraband into my room. Any attempt to explain would serve no purpose other than to assassinate untold minutes of my life.

Safely alone, I pulled the big red bottle of *Raid* from the plastic bag and tried to read the label, written in Spanish.

Only when you first start learning a foreign language do you begin to appreciate the importance of context. Even though I couldn't translate the label, I recognized phrases such as: well-ventilated area; don't get on skin; don't drink; and . . . poison. My ability to recognize these phrases would become extremely useful in the months ahead.

Taking the warnings on the bottle to heart, I opened up the two-foot by two-foot sliding-glass window in my room; stripped my sheets from my mattress; lifted the mattress from the narrow bed, which consisted of wooden planks instead of springs. That done, I propped the mattress against the wall that held my single window.

I stepped back to admire my work.

The mattress leaned where I had put it, virtually humming with bed bug activity. Little did the creatures know that their Armageddon was at hand.

I popped the lid off the red bottle and pulled the safety pin. As I touched the "fire" button, a white cloud of toxic smoke issued from a small plastic nozzle. This cloud hit the mattress, bounced off, and ricocheted back into the room.

The bitter, acrid taste of *Raid* fouled my tongue. My eyes watered. I began wheezing as the stuff pushed the oxygen out of my blood cells on its trip to my hapless, vulnerable brain.

The mattress itself went into convulsions as if it were a living being, rather than host to a settlement of insects.

Working quickly, I pulled my shirt up over my nose for safety, then made several long passes across the mattress with the spray bottle, leaving a checkerboard of slightly damp streaks to mark the treated area. When I was done with the first side, I flipped the mattress over and did the same on its backside. To be safe, I also doused the edges.

When I was done, the toxic haze was so thick you couldn't see the wall on the other side of the room. My eyes burned and watered. I lifted my pillow case and attempted to fan the toxic cloud toward the window, to little avail. Eventually I decided to leave and go for a walk for a few hours.

Marisol gave me a perplexed look as I slammed my door to stop the white *Raid* clouds from escaping.

"Bye!" I gasped in English, one of the few words she understood. She waved at me, and I went out.

Within forty-five minutes, I could breathe normally again. I continued my day, enjoying the breeze off the Pacific ocean. I walked down to Larcomar, a mall nestled into the Costa Verde with a great view of the churning waters below. From there, I made my way back up Avenida Larco to the Ovalo de Miraflores, where major roads intersected at the unofficial center of Miraflores. When night fell, I returned home.

Marisol was nowhere to be seen as I entered. I could sneak in. What a relief! I opened the door to my room. The mattress was still hanging sadly against the wall, next to the open window.

The toxic smell persisted, but not so chokingly intense.

I pulled the mattress down. The ticking felt moist to the touch. I threw the mattress back on the bed frame above the wooden planks and dressed it with sheets, pillows, and blankets. White specks floated lazily to the floor every time I slapped the surface of the mattress, but otherwise the room was unchanged.

I lay down to sleep. My rest was undisturbed. I had no welts on my skin then or thereafter.

The bed bugs were dead and, after a week of dizziness from the residual fumes of the *Raid*, everything was perfect in Lima once more.

Chapter 5

My Cousins Who Hanged a Kid

I needed to learn Spanish.

Minimal research directed me to classes being offered in the center of Lima. The classes were designed to accommodate foreigners residing in Perú, at a cost of S/. 150 per month. This was about the equivalent of $50, and since the classes lasted one month with no obligation to continue, I felt it was too good an opportunity to pass up.

Still not confident using the S/. 1 micro-buses or taxies, I decided to hike to the center of Lima. The hike would allow me to familiarize myself with local landmarks which would be useful if I ever again found myself wandering around clueless in those neighborhoods.

Armed with yet another foolproof plan, I headed down the central boulevard of Avenida Arequipa, one of the major spokes leading from the Ovalo de Miraflores. The street had a nice walking path in its middle, lined with regular shade trees to make the journey pleasant. On either side of the path, cars and buses hurtled by in the frantic daily rat race.

After more than three hours of walking, I reached the center of Lima. I had ripped a map from a phone book, and on it I found the small side street that led to my destination. The school, called the Idiomas Catholica, sat right behind Plaza Francia.

A few steps later, I climbed the school's steps and knocked on the door.

"Hello," I said into a little window that opened up above me. "I was told you have classes here for tourists?"

A tough, elderly lady with silver hair gazed down her nose at me. After a moment, she slammed the window shut and opened the door.

"Right this way," she said.

I stepped up and over the threshold, following her into her office, where she sat me down. Then she handed me a piece of paper.

"What's this?"

"A placement test."

My spirits sank. If there was one thing I was sick of, it was exams.

College exams.

Aptitude exams.

Placement exams.

Exams you paid $100 for.

Exams you paid $200 for.

Exams you paid $300 for, as well as another $150 for a study manual produced by the same company that made the exam.

I was good at exams, but by now found them demeaning. Exams were like lie-detector tests: People only took the results seriously if you failed.

I eyeballed the silver-haired woman's paper with contempt; then I started scribbling. In ten minutes flat, I finished. "Done," I said.

She looked up from her desk and took my proffered paper. She examined my work for a moment. "Looks like you need a basic class," she said.

I nodded. *That's what I would have told you if you had asked, instead of giving me a test.*

She led me downstairs. On this floor were two teachers who gave classes to tourists.

"I'll have you sit in for one lecture with each teacher, and you can pick the one you like better."

I agreed.

The first lecture room was a typical classroom. There were about twenty desks aligned in neat and tidy rows, with twelve or thirteen students all seated toward the front. From their clothing I guessed about half the students were American, while the rest were foreigners from a variety of nations. The classroom's walls were the same shade of green that you find in a mental ward, and the fluorescent lights illuminated it with a hum and an almost imperceptible flicker designed to slowly drive you crazy over time.

This teacher's name was Esperanza. She had a beehive hairdo and wore glasses with wingtip frames.

"New student," my silver-haired guide said, and walked away without another word.

Esperanza nodded and indicated that I should take a seat. I found a place and settled in as quickly as possible. I sensed that my arrival was a grand and unwelcome interruption, and the feeling made me uncomfortable. When I was quietly seated, a student resumed reading aloud from a book. The other twelve students bowed their heads to follow along in their own copies while Esperanza stared holes through an identical tome at the front of the class. Every second or so, Esperanza corrected the student's halting pronunciation. Her interruptions came so frequently that the student started to stutter.

I began flashing back to my college days. My college career had been a series of stops and starts. I'd go to school for a while, then quit and drift from job to job for a few months before returning. Sitting in classes in those days, I'd been prone to panic attacks.

I'd huddle in the back row, feeling that I didn't belong there, paranoid that my presence would be discovered and that secret police would come to march me out and cast me to the curb.

Sometimes I would feel myself sinking down, down, down through clinking ceramic floor tiles. The sharp edges pinched, scratched, and shifted unpredictably as I scrambled for purchase in my desperate attempt to escape oblivion. Returning to such an environment was not a welcome turn of events.

"That's enough," Esperanza commanded in English to the student trying to read for her. The heads of all the other students lifted up in silent unison. The snap of Esperanza's voice roused me from my reflections. Her gaze fixed on me like a gun turret. "New guy, start reading!" Her thick Spanish accent almost rendered the words unintelligible.

One of the other students hastily offered me a book turned to the correct page. He was a thin, nervous-looking guy, and as I nodded in thanks he bobbed his head as if to say, "good luck."

Once I found my place, I began to speak the first words.

"Stop!" Esperanza shouted. She then corrected my pronunciation.

I began again.

"Stop!" she screamed again.

My eye twitched. A small crack appeared in my mental wall. Esperanza seemed to enjoy the discomfort she caused her students.

I looked at her for a moment, considering whether or not I should strike back. I decided it wasn't worth it. She seemed to be one of those people who labor to sow the seeds of discord even while steadfastly declaring an enduring love of harmony. Experience has shown me that there is no way to engage that personality type and emerge victorious. I closed the book with a thud.

Esperanza simply stared at me.

"This isn't working," I said. "Where's the other class?"

Esperanza froze, speechless.

The other students sat still, looking back and forth from me to Esperanza. The one who'd been stuttering aloud looked sympathetic. The weird thing was, these students all were adults. Obviously they thought pain and humiliation were prerequisites to education.

Why?

Eventually, Esperanza found her voice and her poise, pointing vaguely toward the door before she gestured toward the thin student who had lent me his book, commanding him to read aloud. He complied with haste as I picked up my things and left.

I was relieved to go. I'd had enough of classrooms that focused more on obedience than education. Learning is empowerment; obedience is submission. I couldn't conceive of a scenario where the two conflicting objectives could mutually exist. Even so, I had not properly field tested my notion, and I felt a sense of failure even as I rejected the commonly accepted model of instruction.

Not knowing where to go next, I began looking for a classroom populated by tourists.

The hallway was open to the sky. The building that housed the school had four walls but no roof; in its center was an open-air courtyard.

Being outside helped me collect myself again.

After a while I found the tourist class; this class did not meet in a room, but in a gazebo with open doors on either end to let the wind blow through.

This teacher noticed me walking toward her group. She beckoned. She was an elderly redhead with a slight frame and a quick smile.

"Are you looking for a Spanish class?" she asked me in Spanish.

"Yes," I replied.

"Excellent, I'm Luz Marie. Please take a seat."

In the class were two other travelers: Dietmar, a fortyish guy from Germany who oddly reminded me of Homer Simpson; and Hiro, a young man from South Korea.

"Class, we have a new student," Luz Marie said.

I waved.

They waved back.

I sat down.

This classroom had an old Spanish feel, and the wide-open double doors on either end produced a sensation of freedom. In fact, I might have been sitting in a miniature version of the Coliseum. I felt as if I were taking a lesson at the entry hall, just next to the gates of Mt. Olympus.

As I settled back, I began to drift off into the standard half-asleep mental state I had been conditioned to adopt in all classroom settings. Semi-hibernation allowed me to tolerate the inevitable lack of stimulation without fidgeting in a way that would become distracting. I did not wish to be the focus of attention.

Luz Marie had other ideas.

"Perhaps you could tell us about yourself?"

Still a bit agitated about the entry test and my experience in Esperanza's class, I scrunched up my lips. "I'm from the US." I used the Spanish phrases with which I was most familiar. "I have a brother and a sister. Where I'm from, it is very cold —"

"Stop, stop, stop," Luz Marie said. "You make it too easy for yourself. I'm sure you've used that dialogue a million times."

I shrugged.

"Let's try something different," she said with a smile. "Tell us a story from your childhood."

Silence fell. All eyes were on me.

I had to think. I wasn't ready . . .

I looked around the room, expecting to be assaulted by fluorescent lights and sea-foam-green paint. Their absence and the soft breeze blowing through the gazebo calmed me.

"We're waiting," reminded Luz Marie.

I cleared my throat, riffling through my memories. Tell them a story. I chose one from years gone by; an experience which had, perhaps, done more to prepare me for travel than any other in my life.

"I can only think of one; it's from when I was young."

"Go on."

"I'm not sure I have the vocabulary." I tried to start, but I couldn't. I realized there was a word I needed that I simply didn't know. "Um, how do you say . . . when you want to kill somebody?"

Luz Marie's eyes twinkled, but she didn't object. She gave me the Spanish verb for "to kill," which is *matar*.

But *matar* wasn't the word I was looking for. I was thinking of a specific kind of killing. "No," I said, "when you *matar* somebody with a rope."

I lifted one hand over my head and made a jerking motion. Then I tilted my head sideways and stuck out my tongue.

"Oh," Luz Marie said, "the verb for 'to hang' is *colgar*."

"Great," I said. I cleared my throat once more. "When I was young, about ten or so, a couple of my cousins decided to *colgar* somebody."

Hiro and Dietmar stared, but nobody said anything.

"These were my rowdy cousins, who had grown up in Kentucky. I played with them a lot, although when I was with them, I often feared something terrible would happen. I suppose this fear was helpful, because it scared me into adopting a respectful attitude. The one thing my cousins from Kentucky couldn't stand was being disrespected."

I stuttered as I searched for words, but Luz Marie was surprisingly good at supplying me with the correct phrases when I floundered too long, and never in a way that impeded my presentation. Attempting narrative, I gained momentum, speaking my Spanish with greater fluency.

"The kid's name was Darren, and he was kind of arrogant. I can't remember exactly what he did, but he'd annoyed my cousins, Trevor, Billy, and Cole."

As I continued to talk, I found myself forgetting that I was communicating in a different language. I fell back into the story to relive the moment as if it were happening once again:

*

The day was cold, in early autumn. Leaves were starting to take color, and the air was harsh and crisp.

The five of us had been playing out back, far enough from the house that none of our parents could see us.

That was, of course, the point.

But Darren had gone a little too far with his freedom, and now he found himself the center of the other boys' ire.

"We've had enough of your attitude, Darren," Cole said.

"Oh yeah?" Darren scoffed. "Well, what are you going to do about it?"

"We're going to hang you," Trevor snapped.

With that, Darren blanched, but what could he do? Darren had no allies. Trevor, Billy, and Cole were brothers. Darren was a cousin from the other side of the family. That side of the family was large enough that perhaps the loss of Darren wouldn't be missed; at least, that seemed to be the implication. I could have taken Darren's side, but I feared piping up for Darren might put me at risk for a hanging as well.

Trevor pulled a rope from his satchel. He was of the age where he didn't go anywhere without a rope. In his free time he liked to practice tying nooses exactly for moments like these, and he'd gotten quite good at it. Trevor set to work as Cole and Billy led Darren to one of those giant propane tanks that rise up about four feet off the ground. Most of the houses where I grew up had propane tanks out back for winter heating. This particular propane tank was conveniently close to a tree with a low-hanging branch.

"Get up there!" Cole barked.

"No! I'm not going up there!" Darren replied.

"Get up there now!" Trevor yelled.

Darren got up there.

"Now take this," Trevor ordered, throwing Darren the noose. Darren caught it. He was facing away from the tree, so he didn't see Cole throw the other end of the rope over the branch. The rope landed on the ground with a thud, and Cole just looked at it. He didn't run over and pick it up or fasten it to anything. The rope just lay there in the dirt. I gave him a quick glance, and he winked at me.

That's when I realized it was all a practical joke.

They weren't fastening the rope to anything. Darren would step off the propane tank and fall to the ground, shaken but otherwise unhurt. What was coming might be an intense object lesson for a ten-year-old, but at least Darren wouldn't die.

I looked back to Darren, still arrogant and defiant; this attitude had gotten him into my cousins' bad graces in the first place.

"Put the rope over your neck!" Billy yelled.

"No!"

"Do it, or we'll do worse to you."

Darren knew my cousins well enough to believe it, although I was hard pressed to think of something worse than getting hanged.

He put the noose over his neck.

"Now, jump!"

Darren seemed on the verge of objecting again, but perhaps inspiration struck him. With an impulsive leap, he sprang high into the air, hands outstretched and, still in mid-air, dove and spun, seeking the other end of the dangling rope — his salvation. In his deranged terror, he thought that if he could just grab the other end of the rope, he could pull himself to safety: a colossal miscalculation. Darren's fingers closed around the rope, causing his body weight to pull the noose tight around his neck. Rather than fall unharmed to the ground, Darren began choking.

"*Gaaaackkk!*" Darren exclaimed, while his feet began to dance like the tail of a strung-up fish. His fingers were locked in a death grip around the dangling end of the rope as he swayed back and forth; his weight pulled the noose ever tighter around his neck.

"Let go of the rope, you idiot!" Trevor yelled.

"You're choking yourself, you fool!" Cole screamed.

"You're going to die," Billy shouted.

But Darren was determined. Desperate, he clutched at the rope tightening around his neck. His cheeks turned blue. His eyes began bulging.

Eventually my cousins did the only thing they could: they beat Darren until he let go of the rope and fell, relatively uninjured, to the ground.

"Darn fool," they would say later, "dang near choked himself to death on a rope that wasn't tied to anything."

*

When I'd finished the story for my Spanish class, I looked around at Luz Marie's other students, saying: "That's how I learned to keep a low profile."

Luz Marie's eyes twinkled as she looked at me.

"Class," she said, glancing at her other two students, "you know how we're always losing students after only one session because they think we're too crazy?"

Dietmar and Hiro grinned wolfishly.

"Somehow, I don't think we're going to lose *him*." Luz Marie tilted her head toward me.

With that, the three of them broke out laughing.

"His cousins used to *hang* kids for fun," Hiro said, guffawing so hard his eyes watered.

I chuckled too.

As the others laughed, Luz Marie leaned forward.

"Very fluent storytelling," she said with a wink.

Only then did I realize how much she had coached me through the narrative. I was momentarily stupefied by the effectiveness of her gentle guidance.

Luz Marie started gathering up her bags. I glanced at my watch, it was still early.

"Where are we going?"

"We're going around the corner to get some pisco sours," Luz Marie said with a smile. "I find my students can speak with greater ease after they've had one."

I knew what a pisco sour was. Pisco is Perú's national alcoholic beverage, a colorless grape brandy guaranteed to improve every situation. Pisco sours are Perú's national drink and all travelers to Perú fall in love with them after the first sampling. The prospect of combining Spanish class with such a charming beverage was appealing on a fundamental level.

I had found my classroom.

Chapter 6

Total Immersion

One morning, I woke to find myself staring into the eyes of the world's largest cockroach. The roach was sitting on the floor next to my bed, sniffing around for crumbs. The thing looked like some expensive crustacean you might pay fifty dollars for at a five-star restaurant. The two antennae on top of its head twirled in opposite directions.

I stared at him.

He stared back.

I felt a strange connection, as if this insect were defying the natural order and about to speak.

I could nearly hear its words: *"I am the superior life form here. All your creature comforts belong to me."*

I lifted myself from the mattress as slowly and as silently as I could. The cockroach's antennae followed my motion.

How do I kill you? I thought. The last thing I wanted to do was crush such a huge cockroach with my hand. The thought of having sticky bug innards all over my palm filled me with revulsion. I glanced around, and my eyes came to rest upon my shoes.

Ah, the shoe: the tried and true weapon of cockroach killers everywhere.

I reached slowly for a shoe. My fingers inched along the carpet.

The shoe was just out of reach. I stretched. . . .

The antennae swiveled.

The insect was on to me!

With a lunge, I dove out of bed in a frontal roll. Then I spun, reversed direction, and leaped through the air, bringing the shoe down in a violent arc.

The cockroach was off in a blinding sprint. It's terrifying how fast they move, scurrying off toward any crack or crevice they can scuttle into. If you have an imagination, the thought of where a cockroach can hide itself can be absolutely mortifying.

I knew I couldn't live in this room knowing that cockroach was still alive.

Down came my shoe, clipping the cockroach on the back end and killing approximately thirty percent of him.

But seventy percent of a cockroach can live a long and happy life, and the rest of the insect continued on its desperate run to the safety of the wall with only the slightest reduction in speed.

Adrenaline sparked my agility, and I loaded my shoe to fire again.

Blam!

Blam!

Blam!

Three times I hammered the floor, each time catching an antenna, limb, or wing. With the fourth hit, the vile bug stopped moving.

I rolled over into a sitting position and wiped my brow with my forearm.

The deed was done.

I felt suddenly helpless. A series of strange flashbacks to my childhood flooded my mind. With startling clarity, I remembered playing in the woods of Northern Wisconsin and coming across a bees' nest in the woods, then finding a wood tick burrowing into my arm. Wood ticks were a dangerous nuisance for anyone who spent time outside — but I hadn't given them a thought in decades. Yet now I could see the tick's legs, its fat blood-filled belly . . .

Shaking my head to clear it of unwelcome memories, I decided a shower would help. I scraped the remains of the cockroach into a plastic bag, making every effort not to let the crackly shell contact with skin. Then I threw the bag into the garbage, put the garbage outside, and tried to forget that the incident had ever happened.

Into the shower.

A shower always helps.

Ignoring the frigid temperature of the water, I soaked for a while.

When I was finished and dressed, I made my way to the kitchen.

Marisol and Jocelyn were sitting there, already munching on their morning bread. They were dressed informally in worn sweatshirts and pants. The kitchen was small, with one rickety table surrounded by counters and a gas stove. Crude tubes went from the stove to a propane tank. The two of them sat on either side of the small table, and they smiled at me as I entered. The obvious resemblance between mother and daughter in both their appearance and their mannerisms made for a pleasant scene.

"Good morning," they said, almost in unison.

"Good morning."

I debated whether or not to tell them about my recent death match with the insect. Initially, I decided against it, but the quiet in the room changed my mind.

"There was a cockroach," I said, beginning my story.

Marisol tilted her head in complete non-comprehension. "*Que*?"

"A cockroach," I repeated, making my fingers into antennae.

Jocelyn laughed.

Marisol looked even more confused.

"A . . ." I paused. For a moment, it didn't feel like I was in a kitchen in Perú anymore. The strange, vibrant memory of my childhood returned to overlay it all. Plush, green wilderness surrounded me, in the midst of pine and oak trees on a dewy Wisconsin summer morning.

"What are you trying to say?" I heard Marisol ask, but somehow she sounded like my mother.

The displacement was potent and mesmerizing.

Images from my youth overswept me, stimulated

by the frustration of not being able to make myself understood. I was using parts of my mind that had lain dormant for a long time, and the effort stirred up thoughts that almost preceded the awareness of consciousness.

I looked down at my hands and could see a ghost-image: the chubby fingers of a child.

"Excuse me," I said, leaving the kitchen and retiring to my room. I wanted to engage the illusion without distraction.

Alone again, I let myself fall into my past.

Abruptly I was exploring a wood pile that dominated our yard for a summer. The planks were the raw material for an addition to our home, but I saw only a massive labyrinth for adventure and exploration.

I shuffled through the small spaces made by the haphazard stacks of logs. The more rational part of my mind now recognized how dangerous this had been then. Any sudden shift of the crude structure might have left me trapped or seriously injured. But I pushed that line of thinking away.

It was just a memory.

I was safe in a memory.

As a little boy, I didn't think of consequences or danger, only of satisfying my curiosity.

Inside the log there were creatures and insects — insects like the cockroach.

In Lima, the day passed, while everything I did brought back some vivid recollection from childhood. A thousand forgotten images came alive. Memories long locked away, lost in a sense, came forth due to the strangeness of my new surroundings. The exotic culture of Perú shook my thought patterns free from where they had settled, and gave a new twist to anything and everything I could recall.

I basked in it.

I found that revisiting old memories changes their nature. The advantage of an adult perspective takes the sting out of old wounds. Words remembered as being spoken in anger are revealed, upon examination, to be no more than a friendly jest. Revisiting instances of harbored guilt often expose that the action was not taken as a cruelty. All our perceptions are magnified in the moment and distorted by the mists of memory. The passage of time reveals we are neither as good nor as evil as we might have come to believe.

Such exploration is liberating.

Chapter 7

Unnecessary Risks

Perú was inexpensive. I had saved up a little bit of money back in the US, but what I needed was time. Perú gave me the opportunity to stretch my meager cupful of minutes into a vast ocean.

The $120 fee for my room included everything, with heat and water and cable TV included in the base price.

Transportation was inexpensive as well, and as my Spanish fluency increased, more options became available to me. I could get around town by *combi* for one nuevo sol, S/. 1, which was about the equivalent of a quarter USD. If I wanted to go by taxi, I'd be spending two or three dollars.

Food was cheap, too. There were many local restaurants that featured a daily menu for S/. 5. This consisted of a drink, soup, main course, and pastry. After eating the *menu*, I generally had no need to eat anything else for the rest of the day.

About once a week, I'd treat myself to a steak special at a little restaurant near the Ovalo de Miraflores. The special included a steak, salad, fries, and a glass of wine for S/. 14.90.

I could go to the movies for S/. 7 — half price on Tuesdays.

Living in Perú took the pressure off me financially, and created the freedom to think about things other than how I was going to cover monthly expenses. I felt I had stumbled into a closeout sale on time, and I wanted to purchase as much as I could.

But Perú had a dark side too: it was important to keep on your toes.

On one occasion, walking through the park on a sunny afternoon, a taxi came flying around the corner way too fast. By then, I was used to the frantic traffic of Lima, but this was excessive even by those standards. I dived out of the road and onto the grass as the taxi sped by, wheels squealing, the whole vehicle weaving back and forth, nearly out of control.

I stood there watching, dazed, wondering what was happening until a police car came screeching out of the narrow streets in hot pursuit. Like the taxi, it skidded around the corners as it followed the vehicle around the park and down a side road at the far end.

I waited, listening for a crash or a siren.

Soon I heard a crack in the distance. With a sickening sensation, I realized that it must have been a gunshot. However, the shot sounded nothing like gunshots in movies. There was no resonance to the sound, just a popping noise that had no directionality as it bounced around the sound-deadening walls of the buildings.

I waited.

No more shots rang out.

For a moment, I was tempted to walk back home and lock myself in my room. But I shook that impulse away. Living in Perú had already emboldened me to seek out new experiences when the opportunity arose. I decided the only action true to the spirit of travel was to go and take a look at what had transpired.

I found it easy to follow the black skid marks the vehicles left on the road, so I trotted along the path in the direction of the gunshot, expecting to see something uncommon. Most photographers and newscast teams arrive minutes or even hours after an event takes place. The scene would be an opportunity to observe the raw, uncensored facts of the altercation before the local media had a chance to begin disseminating their interpretation.

I rounded the corner and came upon the carnage. The taxi sat by the side of the road, its windshield spattered with orange-red droplets.

I looked at the droplets for some time before I realized they were blood.

The blood didn't look like anything I'd ever seen in the movies. For that reason, at first, it didn't seem real.

I made myself study the view for a moment. The shadows in the car seemed to suggest a supine body across the seats, but I did not cross over to have a closer look.

The street was still open; the police yet in the process of taking control. Observing the action left me numb. There didn't appear to be any victory here, only chaos. I didn't see evidence of anything that could indisputably be called good or evil — those details would be added in by others when the story was told.

After a moment I walked on, not happy about what I'd seen.

I concluded that the taxi must have been stolen, since police had pursued it, though I didn't have enough Spanish to confirm my surmise by following the news.

Was it justifiable to shoot a man who had stolen a car? Had there only been one person in the car? That must have been the case since I hadn't seen any evidence of anyone in custody, or further pursuit on the part of the police.

I decided to keep walking to think for a while. Passing the bloody vehicle, I arrived at Benavides. On the main city street, life went on as usual. Cars and *combis* rushed by with horns beeping and people shouting, oblivious to what had just transpired. Day to day life continued without interruption.

I made a long circuit before returning back to my room both physically and emotionally exhausted. My small, confined quarters provided an immediate sense of relief.

This was the age before internet-enabled cell phones, and I instinctively reached toward the TV with the hope of finding some news about the shooting.

I paused with my finger in the air.

Even if there was news, I realized I wouldn't be able to understand the nuance of the language. I left the TV off and went to sit down on the bed. My linguistic barrier had effectively taken me off the grid. My mind, used to constant demands on its attention, started casting out desperately. The sensation was disconcerting. I had to try to steady myself.

What did I need the news for anyway? Hadn't I seen the events unfold with my own eyes? Did I not trust my own senses?

I replayed the scenario in my mind simply because I felt compelled to process what had occurred.

What if I had been in the intersection?

What if there had been a woman pushing a baby carriage across the street?

The car could have run any number of innocent bystanders down.

Something needed to be done.

After thinking for a while, I started to relax. The shooting seemed excessive, but such a thing could have happened anywhere. If statistics are to be believed, the place you're most likely to die is at home in your own bed.

Voices trickled in from the street but my linguistic barrier rendered the sounds into a harmless buzz that I could ignore at my convenience. I was suddenly glad for the increased ability to dampen out sensory intrusions. You don't read words you can't understand, or eavesdrop on conversations you can't comprehend. Avoiding those stimulations created a soothing internal silence.

A touch of vague consternation remained at being left out of the loop, but the sensation steadily faded with every passing moment.

Over the next few weeks I grew more deliberate in the management of my thoughts and activities, and found that a wake up call was exactly what I'd needed. I don't believe I could have gotten that far off the grid based on discipline alone. Sometimes, needless risks have unanticipated benefits.

Chapter 8

Agony Even the Shaman Cannot Cure

As the months dragged on, my adoptive family grew accustomed to my eccentricities. As long as the rent came in on time, I could do as I pleased. They looked out for me as well; I liked knowing people who'd be concerned if I went missing for a while.

I held up my end, too. I didn't bring any visitors to the house, or attract unsavory characters who'd come looking for me to sell or buy intoxicants.

Intoxicants are the real problem among back-packing tenants, especially in a country where drugs are affordable and easily available.

It's surprising how many people come to Perú to lose themselves for years or decades in psychedelic oblivion. You can never tell what people are like by their appearances. One day a guy might seem totally normal, and the next he's wandering the street shirtless, trying to sell the last of his luggage to scrounge up money for a high.

Recreational dabbling can become an all-encompassing way of life. I don't begrudge people their fun, but drugs have a way of going from one person's diversion to somebody else's major problem.

I'd seen it back in my youth, as my hometown turned into a seething meth pit that swallowed up some of my closest friends, who'd gone from promising students to toothless jailbirds. I had to cut them loose, like one climber slitting the safety cord on another to keep himself from being pulled down into the void along with the rest.

The cut had cost me, but I kept my teeth.

I knew I wouldn't fall to drug addiction, even in a country with as many temptations as Perú. I'd spent too much effort cultivating an agile mind to waste it in the pursuit of cheap escape. Marisol seemed to notice this, and her confidence in me grew. She made more of an effort to introduce me to her friends.

One day, a girlfriend of Marisol's invited me to visit her cousin's house out in Ancon.

"Ok," I replied, not knowing where Ancon was, but happy to embark on another random adventure.

We took the number two bus through the center of Lima and onward to the end of the bus line. The old bus rattled along until the sun began to graze the horizon, and the fluorescents outlining the aisle began to glow in the long shadows.

"How much farther?" I asked my guide.

"Not far now," was her reply.

Her response had been the same for the previous two hours.

Down, down, down went the bus, following the great northern highway. Outside, ocean waves crashed against the cliffs.

We abandoned the number two bus and jumped into a *combi*, a little van filled with round-faced people carrying chickens in cages.

I smiled at the other passengers.

They smiled back.

The chickens flapped their wings, their feathers brushing against me through the bars.

The *combi* roared to life and started on its way.

My legs went numb; I had no place to stretch them. Through a rusty hole in the floor, I could see the highway spinning by below.

Away from Lima, life was different. Even in the crimson light of the setting sun, people were still bustling about their tiny roadside shops. There is always a similarity to the decorations of street vendors in South American cities: those people like bright colors, and the vending kiosks look as if the circus has just come to town. Yet the sand in the air abrades everything, and even the bright and new decorations were doomed to fade like the flickering, endless beige canopies surrounding them.

Abandoned stores beside the road lurked like carcasses of fallen beasts, still except for the flapping of the once-bright plastic banners now as dark and old as the desert.

Seeing that state of despair all around, it's impossible not to feel embarrassed about how easy your own life has been. No matter what problems you've faced or what challenges you've overcome, most of us have always had options other than a lifetime sentence of squeezing coins out of a highway kiosk selling cheap plastic trinkets.

The same trinkets everyone else was selling.

Finally we arrived: The house in Ancon was large, some sort of factory with a fenced-in green area out back. The green area was a miniature football field beside a swimming pool on a raised platform.

People were gathered about, drinking.

"This is our new American friend."

A round of applause went up. Genuine cheers of affection. "Have a drink!"

I took the drink and knocked it back.

People came up and tried to talk to me, but I couldn't understand them. I made terrible errors in Spanish, but they just laughed and danced and drank.

I joined them.

The night passed on, eventually dissolving into dreamland.

*

I awoke on a cot in a small room, only vaguely knowing where I was.

When you wake up drunk in a foreign country, it's different from the disorientation you get when you wake up drunk back home.

Back home, you can forget whether you're at your parents' house or at a friend's house. Either way, in the haze of a bleary morning, you can probably estimate where you are.

In a foreign country, the process of elimination takes longer.

Where am I?

The question flashes through your mind. As if by instinct, you divide up the possibilities into bigger swaths of land.

Wisconsin?

No.

This can't be Wisconsin . . . wait, wasn't I on an airplane recently?

The darkness thunders down. It's quite unpleasant until you start making progress. You sift for clues.

Airplane . . .

Yes . . .

I'm on a trip!

I'm out of the United States!

South America!

Perú . . . that's it! Perú.

Once you have a breakthrough, the rest comes back in a flood, and you're left wondering what, exactly, woke you up. In my case, it happened to be an annoying pain in my side.

With the confusion as to my whereabouts resolved, the pain came back with a vengeance.

"Ouch."

I rubbed my stomach. The pain was unusual. It wasn't a bite, or a stab, or a pinch. It was more of an ache. A slow, deep, throbbing ache.

An odd pain, not pronounced, but distressing. Unsettling because it pulsed. It had started as a minor irritation. But now that I was awake, I could tell it was getting worse.

Slowly. Inexorably. Terribly.

Worse.

Any pain is bad, but constant, steady, slowly increasing pain is unbearable.

I sat up and rubbed my side.

The pain persisted.

I stood.

The pain remained.

I lay back down again.

The pain continued on, completely oblivious to my efforts.

"Stupid pain."

I thought for a moment. I was still waking up, so my thought process was groggy, but I could make progress if I worked at it.

After a while, I deduced that the pain was something like the need to go to the bathroom.

I chuckled. That must be it!

I stood up and went downstairs to where I remembered the bathroom to be. I closed the little door and stood over the toilet.

Nothing happened.

I gave the little mental signal to urinate which I had given without fail since before the time I was capable of conscious thought.

Nothing.

In fact, the only thing that happened was that the pain continued to increase.

Now I really had to urinate.

But I couldn't!

Panic set in, but that emotion was useless; I pushed it away. Instead, I went outside and decided to drink some water.

Whatever the blockage was, I thought, I'd push it through by brute force.

I turned on the faucet.

Some little warning bell in the back of my head went off about not drinking the tap water in South America.

I didn't even hesitate.

Pain has a way of overriding cautionary signals.

I gulped down several liters of water and went back to the toilet.

I waited to urinate.

Nothing.

All the while, the pain in my side grew; like a clenched fist of anguish, it poked its long, bony fingers into the darkest recesses of my abdomen.

I lay down by the toilet.

The porcelain was cool. Beads of comforting sweat lined the toilet's bottom.

The pain persisted.

I assessed my situation.

I was in South America, Perú. I didn't know anyone. I couldn't speak the language. I wasn't exactly sure what city I was in, and I was suffering through the most terrible pain I'd ever experienced in my life.

Also, that pain was getting worse.

Finally, I reached the only conclusion I could.

I needed a hospital.

I struggled to my feet and tried to remember the layout of the compound.

I was hesitant to wake this family in the middle of the night. After all, I was as much a stranger to them as they were to me. You never want some wacko walking through your house at two or three in the morning, screaming in anguish.

But what could I do?

I got to the front door and knocked on it.

No response.

I knocked louder.

And kept knocking. Finally, somebody came to the door.

I crumpled. "Hospital," I said.

"Oh my god!" somebody replied.

About now, lights were lit. I could hear voices from every corner, chirping away. I could make out most of what they said.

"What's going on?"

"The gringo, he's sick."

"What's the matter with him?"

"Get the medicine woman!"

Now, I was at the bottom of a poking and prodding huddle of people standing around me, chattering away. Their words became ever more hurried and frantic, soon exceeding my ability to comprehend what was being said.

"Can somebody please take me to a hospital?"

The incomprehensible Spanish conversation surrounding me continued unabated.

An elderly man grabbed a young child and whispered a set of urgent instructions. The child went sprinting off into the night.

"Help is on the way."

"What . . . what about the hospital?"

They shushed me into silence.

Awhile later, a little old woman appeared. She had frazzled gray hair and at least one glass eye. She moved with slow deliberation and balanced on a gnarled cane made from an ancient tree root. She looked at me. With a knotted finger, she poked me in the stomach.

"Ow!"

With that she nodded, and gave some instructions.

"What's going on?" I asked.

"She told us to bring you some tea."

"Tea?" I replied, incredulous. "But I want to go to the hospital!"

"You'll drink the tea."

A few minutes later, I was presented with a scalding-hot cup of tea.

I drank it as fast as I could.

Everybody waited and watched for about thirty seconds.

After thirty seconds, I threw up the tea.

"Can we please go to the hospital now?"

Finally, they acquiesced.

They loaded me into a van, and we were on our way.

Chapter 9

Death by Peanut Butter and Jelly

As we raced along the coast, the morning sunlight tinted the desert landscape red. Much of Perú is rainforest, but the Andes halt the passage of clouds from the east, leaving the coast fairly desolate; tracts of land go for hundreds of miles with very little vegetation to be seen.

I was using every trick I knew to distract myself from the pain in my abdomen. A sensation in your stomach similar to some sort of big-toothed rodent trying to gnaw his way out grabs your attention. But focusing on the discomfort only makes things worse, so I attempted to send my consciousness elsewhere.

I had assumed the hospital was close, but as we made our way down the highway, our travel time approached infinity. I focused on the surroundings, occupying myself with trying to make sense of them. The same proprietors I had noticed the night before were already back at work, opening up the tiny kiosks I'd watched them close the previous evening.

The hospital finally lurched up out of the sand.

Even though the sun had just begun to peek over the horizon, fifty people formed a long line out front.

I stumbled to the end of the line, cowering in the dirt like a dog. The line was heartbreaking. But who was I to jump in front of all these people? Who was I to think my pain was greater than theirs?

"Go ahead," somebody yelled urgently.

"Go to emergency," somebody else said.

Oh yes, in my deluded state I'd forgotten there is such a thing as an emergency room. I struggled to my feet and stumbled forward.

Someone who might have been an orderly, dressed in blue scrubs, led me into a pale green room. The place looked no cleaner than a highway rest area, but I didn't care. I only wanted the agony to stop. Getting worse throughout the drive, this pain now approached unbearable. Yet its intensity continued to increase with every breath I took.

"Make the pain stop," I mumbled. "I don't care if you kill me or dissect me, but make the pain stop."

A doctor came in and had a look at me. He was wearing the same style of blue scrubs as the orderly. The scrubs were spotless and seemed to have been recently pressed. After a few cursory prods, the doctor hoisted a syringe.

The syringe could have been made from a rusty nail as far as I was concerned.

In went the needle.

Time passed slowly with a needle shooting burning liquid into my arm.

I closed my eyes and willed the anguish in my abdomen to leave me in peace. In my mind's eye, a second hand lumbered around a clock face, each moment marked by an agonizing jolt.

Tick by tock, I began to notice the pain retreating.

The closed fist in my stomach began to unclench. I started to feel better.

The doctor had done it, he had performed a miracle, the pain was gone. I slipped off the table and made my way to the bathroom, where I finally could urinate. *Hallelujah!* Suddenly the whole world seemed brighter; life was worth living again.

I'd survived.

But next came the worst part: the consultation.

We went into the doctor's office. The daughter of my host was translating.

They chattered back and forth for a while. The doctor asked questions, and the girl answered them. Nobody looked to me for any clarifications, but occasionally they both looked at me in unison and began to nod knowingly to themselves.

"What —"

"Shhh . . ."

"Excuse me . . ."

"Shhh . . ."

"But maybe I could —"

"Shhhttt!"

Finally, the daughter turned to me.

"We've concluded that the reason you have had this problem is because you've been eating peanut-butter-and-jelly sandwiches."

She spoke the truth: I *had* been eating peanut-butter-and-jelly sandwiches. Considering my problems with the language, I simply didn't always have the energy to face a waiter at a restaurant and try ordering a meal. So I'd gone down to the Wong grocery store and finally found a jar of peanut butter, so I could make peanut-butter-and-jelly sandwiches when I got hungry.

My host's daughter must have told the doctor about my eating habits. Eating PB and J absolutely appalled Peruvians, who are skeptical as to the nutritional value of sandwiches to begin with. A sandwich made out of something bizarre like peanut butter, which is not the table staple in Perú that it is in the States, absolutely couldn't be trusted.

As a result of their concern, my host family and their friends had been conspiring to eliminate my peanut-butter-and-jelly-sandwich eating for some time. This latest illness was an opportunity they couldn't pass up.

"I've had a peanut-butter-and-jelly sandwich every day for the last twenty-five years . . ." I tried to say.

Both the doctor and the girl turned away. The doctor shook his head in disgust. He'd seen it a million times. You try to tell people what will cure them, and they just go into denial.

What can you do with an unreasonable patient who won't give up his peanut-butter-and-jelly sandwiches? A patient on the verge of eating himself into an early grave?

Nothing!

The doctor dusted off his hands and left the room.

Chapter 10

Teaching

Luz Marie made us describe our weekends in class on Monday. My story about the early-morning trip to the hospital was the most dramatic. But even as she chuckled about the events, Luz Marie expressed some real concern over my health.

"My brother is a doctor," she said. "I can take you to see him if you want." Like my host family, she had adopted me.

Something about being a traveler seems to attract generous souls who want only to ease the burdens of a pilgrim's quest. A walking stick is like a banner which calls noble spirits to the cause, and these, in turn, are grateful for the chance to help you carry on. They're out there slumbering, waiting for an opportunity to repay a similar, long-forgotten favor. Without helpers, no traveler would ever finish a journey.

Still, I felt like things were back under control.

"Naw, I seem to be OK now."

"Are you sure?" she asked, unwilling to let the issue drop.

"Yes." I was touched by Luz Marie's display of sincere affection. The warmth with which Peruvians treat each other on a daily basis continues to astonish me. They view Americans with sadness and wonder why we're so cold to one another. Their generosity and sincerity has been something I aspire to integrate into my own character.

The wind kicked up and blew through the open space that functioned as our classroom. Dietmar was depressed because he was rapidly approaching the end of his allotted time in Perú.

Luz Marie didn't understand his consternation. "Why don't you stay?" she asked. "You obviously want to be here. Just extend your trip. Perú is good for you."

Dietmar winced; her words seemed to irritate him. "It's not that simple."

"Sure it is," Luz Marie persisted. "You're an adult. Pick up the phone and cancel your ticket. Or just don't go to the airport."

"It's not that easy," Dietmar snapped. "I need to go back and work."

"Oh, are you out of money?"

"No," Dietmar admitted, "but I can't let a gap develop in my resume that has no explanation."

Luz Marie's face twisted in confusion.

"The job market is very competitive in Germany. If I lose my position, I might never find another."

Luz Marie said nothing, but doubt became plainly visible on her features.

This provoked Dietmar. "You don't know what it's like," he said, losing his cool. "It's not like here, where you can do whatever you want and not worry about the future."

Luz Marie's face hardened, and Dietmar seemed to recognize that his words were unfair even as he spoke them. He settled down.

After a moment, Luz Marie answered. "I think I do know what it's like. I see plenty of travelers with broken spirits such as yourselves." At this she gestured at the three of us. "You come from worlds of intense competition designed to break people down, not build them up; but you've been programmed to think that's how life must be. It isn't. You're allowed to take a break. Trust me when I tell you that you have more options than you realize. Things do tend to work out, even without a specific plan."

Her words seemed to calm Dietmar for the moment.

"Are *you* worried about gaps in your resume?" she said, this time looking at me.

I didn't say anything, but after a moment of reflection I found I had to nod.

"Why?"

"It's what is expected. It's important to develop a resume that shows how every year of your life was dedicated to making you a better employee."

"You believe that?"

I nodded.

"Yet you chose to live here in Perú without any plans to return home?"

I nodded again.

"Isn't that a contradiction?"

I smiled. "Very well, then: I contradict myself."

Luz Marie's eyes widened. There was a long pause, then she replied, "I am large, I contain multitudes."

The quote was from Walt Whitman, which I had clumsily translated into Spanish, so I was somewhat surprised that she'd recognized the lines. We shared a moment of understanding that Dietmar and Hiro observed with confusion.

Finally, Luz Marie spoke again. "I think Perú will be extra good for you." She gave me a wink.

After class, Dietmar was reflective. Hiro wandered off, but Luz Marie asked me to stick around.

"What's your degree in?" she asked.

"English literature."

She nodded as if she expected the answer. "The big risk in studying literature is that you might be tempted to live your life based on the principles you learn."

I laughed.

"It might interest you to know," she continued, "that in addition to teaching here, I also run a language center out in Los Olivos."

I knew where Los Olivos was; I had gone through it on the way to Ancon. It lay on the fringes of Lima.

"Would you like to come and see it? I'm going there now. There might be an opportunity for you."

I shrugged; I didn't have anything else to do.

*

We hiked out of the school toward Calle Alfonso Ugarte. At that time of day, the center of Lima was crowded with vehicles and people.

Alfonso Ugarte is an artery that runs through the heart of a city in the throes of an extreme adrenaline rush. Massive buses hurtle through intersections with little or no regard for the people or animals in their way. Drivers have no qualms about passing within a couple inches of pedestrians as they stand waiting for lights to change. If you're not careful, you can feel the corrugated metal surfaces of the vehicles tickle your clothing as they fly past.

It's not a good street in which to make abrupt or absent-minded changes of direction.

Luz Marie told me she'd normally take a bus, but since there were two of us, it made sense to split a taxi. She hailed one and haggled for a moment before we piled in. Instantly we were off, merging with the ever-pumping, chaotic traffic.

"Have you ever given any thought to teaching?" she asked.

I winced. I got panic attacks while sitting in class as a student; how could I be expected to teach one?

"I don't really want to teach," I said. Ever since I'd announced my plans to get a degree in English, the consensus seemed to be I was destined to become a teacher. It was a fate I purposely avoided.

Luz Marie smiled. "Well, we have a very casual setting in Los Olivos, and the classes only last a month at a time. This would be a good place to try it if you wanted."

I nodded noncommittally.

"The students are very appreciative of having a native speaker for a teacher."

"Um-hmm."

"Plus, you're going to be very popular with the girls."

That got my attention. "Excuse me?"

"This isn't a high school," Luz Marie clarified. "This is a language center for professionals. Most of the students are between twenty and thirty."

Intriguing.

"And they're going to like you."

I laughed at that, but Luz Marie fixed me with a serious look.

"All I'll have to do is walk you through the school, and I'll have a bunch of girls asking to sign up for classes you teach. Remember, you're the exotic foreigner with the accent . . . the type of character they see in romance movies."

That left me a little dumbfounded. I had been so star-struck by all the beautiful people around me that I'd forgotten I was actually the exotic one.

Our taxi pulled into Luz Marie's school, and we climbed out into the street.

The school was built like a fort. It was a solid, brick construction that had been painted dark blue with pleasing gold highlights around the windows and along the tops of the walls. In the center, there was an open patio. Around this were four levels of classrooms stacked one upon the other, with stairways and aisles encircling the whole structure. To my Wisconsin-born eyes, the building looked only half completed. It was odd to see students lounging against a waist-high wall on the third level overlooking the patio. Here there was no protection from rain or snow, and I had to remind myself that it never snowed and only rarely rained.

Luz Marie walked me through the courtyard.

What she had said was true: pretty girls loitered all around.

We went to her office and sat down. She regarded me with a smile.

"Wait a minute," I said. "So are you only teaching at the center of Lima to recruit native speakers to come and teach at your school?"

Her face split wide into a chipmunk-like grin, and she nodded as she chuckled at her inside joke.

"Shanghai them is more like it," I mumbled.

She only continued to laugh. "Naturally, we aren't going to bother with visas. We'll just pay you in cash under the table."

"So it's going to be totally illegal?"

"Yup."

That did it.

"OK," I said. "I'll give teaching a go. When do I start?"

Once again, I felt myself being swept along without control of my destiny, but that was all right, as long as the journey continued.

Chapter 11

One Minute of Prep Time

The next day I returned to Los Olivos to begin my first day of teaching. At the Los Olivos bus stop, there was access to a foot tunnel that went under the Panamericana Norte. Wind blew through the tunnel, kicking up a cloud of discarded tickets that had been dropped by hurrying travelers. At the end of the tunnel was a stairway with a collection of people selling homemade red gelatin, or sugar water in plastic bags. Sometimes there would be a dog sleeping in the corner, sometimes a person, curled up on a piece of cardboard.

Beyond the bus stop, buildings lined the streets; on every block were assortments of internet cafes. Kids exchanged handfuls of nuevo soles for the chance to immerse themselves for countless hours in images of a bouncing hallway seen through the scope of a digitally rendered assault rifle. Modem speakers replicated the sound of gunfire, made tinny by the cheap equipment, and the sound spilled out from between the bars on the windows along with admonishments from the game's control center.

"You lose," it would bellow, or, more disturbingly, "Terrorists win."

These phrases were repeated endlessly. It was impossible not to wonder if anyone ever emerged victorious from the games.

Walking along, I grasped the strap of my backpack on my left shoulder. Another store display had grabbed my interest when I was abruptly distracted by a jerk on my wrist, followed by the sound of tearing Velcro. Not knowing what was happening, I looked up to see a man sprinting down the street.

My left wrist was scratched.

In the place where my watch normally rested was now only a patch of untanned white skin.

The guy had stolen my Timex Ironman!

For a moment, I debated chasing him. Then I thought better of it. After all, it was only a cheap watch, and I'd had it for about five years. Besides, the theft might only be a provocation intended to trick me into giving chase. The thief's real objective might be to lure me into a dark alley, where his friends were waiting to relieve me of all my remaining valuables.

No, the watch was a small price to pay. In a heartbeat, I decided to let it go. I continued watching the thief as I reflected.

He suddenly turned around to look at me. Seeing that I wasn't chasing him, he stopped running and began to walk along casually. He turned his head in the direction he was going and seemed to forget about me.

Now *that* I could not take. If a guy was going to rob me, he should at least have the courtesy to run to the end of the street!

I broke into a run. I was pretty fast because of daily jogs. Adrenaline streaked through me as I realized I was about to start a fight. I'd nearly caught up with the guy and was wondering what I was going to do to him when he happened to look back over his shoulder.

His eyes went wide as he saw me barreling down on him. Once I closed the distance, I realized I was quite a bit taller and thicker than he was. He started running, but it was obvious in a step or two that he wouldn't be able to outdistance me. His face screwed up, as if he were thinking.

He spun around to face me, and abruptly tossed me back my watch.

I caught my watch in the air and stopped.

The guy was waiting, but backing up slowly.

I began backing up, too.

Finally, I turned around and headed on my way, glancing around behind me in case the would-be thief chased after me, this time with knife or gun in hand.

It didn't happen.

The rest of the journey passed without incident, and I arrived at the school out of breath and shaking a little, but none the worse for wear.

"Who are you?" the plump secretary said, gazing at me over her horn-rimmed glasses.

"I'm the teacher." I began telling her what had just happened, but she cut me off.

"Oh, OK," she replied, "here are your books, the room is over there, class starts in one minute."

"Uh . . ." I said, but she pushed me out of the room before I had a chance to ask any questions.

My heart was still pounding from the attempted robbery as I glanced at the packet of books the secretary had given me, which included a workbook and a teacher's book. The teacher's book presumably contained lessons, etc., but I had no idea how it was laid out.

Oh, well.

I stepped into the class. Some students had already arrived and were milling uncertainly. They were two very attractive young women with brown eyes and jet black hair. In fact, their hair was so black it almost looked like they had blue highlights. They smiled at me before sliding into two seats at the very front of the classroom, never taking their gaze off me or dropping their smiles.

I nodded at them and flipped through the teacher's book. In the thirty seconds I had left before class started, I couldn't calm my nerves enough to make sense of what I was looking at. I tossed the teacher's book aside and had a look at the workbook.

The verb "to be."

OK, that was easy enough.

Some kind of bell rang in the distance, and the students made their way to their seats and gazed up at me expectantly.

Darn it! Here I was — teaching! The thing I'd always studiously avoided. My fingers shook, and I couldn't tell if it was from the attempted theft or from a fear of public speaking.

"Hello students, how are you?"

Blank stares.

"Have any of you had any English classes before?"

Blank stares again, and now the students were exchanging confused glances with one another. That wasn't a good sign.

I glanced down at my book again. It said "Basic One" on the cover.

This was their first English class!

I went to the board.

"My . . . name . . . is . . ." I said as I wrote the words on the white board.

The students looked at me. I lifted up a pen and pantomimed that they should be writing their names on their papers.

Thirty little light bulbs went off as the students dug out their notebooks from their backpacks. It's amazing that students always leave their notebooks in their backpacks until they're told they need them. They tote the notebook to class every day but, unless you ask them, you'll never see one. However, once you get them writing on the pages, things get easier. That, at least, was a task they were familiar with.

I went through the class and had them all tell me their names in English. Bit by bit, I began to calm down.

With more pantomimes and crude drawings, I explained a half dozen phrases and verb tenses. Amid giggling and a lot of playing, the students all stayed on task. I avoided speaking in Spanish at all costs. After all, these students were paying to listen to English, weren't they? Therefore, the more English they heard, the more valuable the class would be for them.

The first class went surprisingly fast; and when the bell rang, they certainly knew without me having to tell them that it was time to pack up everything and head out the door.

"Bye-bye, teacher," they said, smiling.

"See you next time."

They pitched out a couple of the other phrases I'd exposed them to in our first class together.

It seemed as if they'd picked up a couple of things, at least.

When they all were gone, I looked down at my watch and realized I hadn't strapped it back on my wrist yet. I pulled the watch from my pocket and sat heavily in the teacher's chair. I finally had a chance to compose myself.

My first class had been such a whirlwind, it had almost seemed like a fantasy.

In a weird way I was almost grateful to the thief for providing me with the distraction necessary to get me through.

Chapter 12

Ivan and the Army of 30 Men

The bus ride to Los Olivos was long, and I habitually visited the English pub in Miraflores when I got home. This wasn't the English pub on Pizza St., but the other English pub that's right behind the Saga Falabella, one of those places with black wooden beams framing whitewashed walls, and flags from various countries hanging down all over the place.

Kyle, a fellow teacher also from the US, introduced me to the joint. Behind the bar were a couple of waitresses who were sisters, and these two enchanted him. One of the sisters, Valeria, caught your attention even though it was hard to pinpoint why. Some girls have that talent. Valeria was always surrounded by a group of onlookers whom she managed expertly.

One day I sauntered into the bar and Shelia, Valeria's sister, came trotting over.

"Be careful," she said with a smile.

"Why?"

"Do you see that big guy?" She nodded in the direction of a large fellow draped over the bar like a bearskin rug.

"Yes."

"His name is Ivan. He's the son of the Yugoslavian ambassador to Perú, and he doesn't like Americans."

"Oh," I said.

I ordered my beer and sat there drinking. Shelia and Valeria came over to chat from time to time, and I hoped some of my other friends would stop by. But that night, all I had was Ivan. And Ivan didn't like Americans.

Ivan kept drinking, too. He was an exceptionally good drinker. When he talked he belted out phrases in a thick Eastern-bloc accent, sounding like an actor in a European gangster movie. We stayed in our designated corners and drank.

But you can't keep to yourself at a bar; that's the whole point. Eventually Ivan decided he needed more of an audience than just the two waitresses and the motley crowd in the place who were totally forgettable.

"Hey, my friend, how do you know deeze girlz?" he suddenly bellowed at me while gesturing at Valeria and Shelia.

"Just from coming in for drinks."

"What iz it dat you do?"

"I teach English, mostly."

He swiveled his seat to face me. His great gorilla chest took up space like Hemingway's must have. He pulled a cigarette from his pocket and then was grasping a pistol. This startled me at first until I realized it wasn't a pistol; it was a cigarette lighter in the shape of a pistol.

"Da real one iz in de car," he said. He lit his cigarette and took a long drag. "And where are you from?"

Shelia and Valeria blanched at the question. Shelia even shook her head at me as if it were better for me to lie. But I thought I'd appeal to the Godfather-type aura Ivan was trying for.

"I can't lie to you, Ivan, I'm from the US."

"Ahhh, zo you know my name."

"Everybody knows your name."

He seemed to appreciate this and sucked on his cigarette contemplatively. "Let me azk you one more ting. What do you tink of the politics of your country?"

I thought about this for a moment and then responded with caution: "I love my country and am disappointed in my government, just like everybody in every country in the world."

At this, Ivan's hard face turned into a wide smile. "Dis iz very good!" he cried, leaping to his feet. He slapped me hard on the back and pulled his stool closer.

The waitresses and the barman at the other end of the room sighed. Ivan was one of those ticking time bombs that could go off at any moment. Any reprieve was a tremendous relief. Ivan ordered some beers and started telling stories. "When I was living in Mexico, I had a dangerous ting happen," he said. "I was driving along in my car and I stopped at a light. A man ran up to me and shoved a gun through the window into my face."

"My goodness. What did you do?" Valeria asked.

"I did the only ting I could do. I grabbed his arm and hit ze gas!"

This bear of a man frantically grabbing a thief by the arm while attempting to accelerate away was the most absurd image I could imagine. I laughed.

Ivan continued: "Of course, he started shooting, and tank God my girlfriend wasn't in ze car with me because he shot ze passenger seat all to hell!"

Ivan chuckled to himself and let his words drift into silence. He always picked random moments to end his stories, and he would pretend not to hear you if you asked for clarifications. It was as if he had taken the mantra 'keep them wanting more' to a ridiculous extreme that resulted in an absolute failure to achieve any kind of resolution whatsoever.

We kept drinking.

When it got late, Ivan decided to invite every-body over to his house. There were only four or five of us by then.

"In the car with the guns?" I asked.

Occasionally, you'd say something that made Ivan very happy. This was one of those times. "Yes, ze guns!"

We piled into the car and headed out on one of those dreamy, half-drunk early morning rides through the lights and darkness of a cold, electric foreign city. After an indeterminable amount of time, we arrived at a mansion behind a locked gate. The house was made entirely of glass and had a swimming pool with an intense reflection that tinted everyone's legs blue up to their knees.

It was a posh place.

Perhaps Ivan really was the son of the ambassador from Yugoslavia. Well, there were ways to find that out.

"Ivan," I asked — and it happened to be one of the occasional times he condescended to hear me — "where did you learn English?"

He took his cigarette out of his mouth. "Prison!" he cried, and then went back to serving himself a drink.

When we all had drinks in hand and had found a place to sit or lounge near the highly reflective pool, Ivan stood before us.

"Let me tell you a story of when I was in ze Dominican Republic. I was living on dis ranch with two girls who called me Don Ivan. It was ze best time of my life! Every day I would stand around on ze ranch with a big white cowboy hat. Every night we would . . . well, never mind . . ."

Ivan looked momentarily befuddled as if he had forgotten his audience contained a pair of girls he was trying to impress. But he quickly collected himself and continued. "There was a *ranchero* there who had just lost his entire ranch to zome bandits. He came up to me one day with a sad look. 'Don Ivan,' he said, 'help me, dey have taken my farm.'"

Ivan shook his whiskey and ice so that it clinked and then drank before looking back at us.

"I looked at dis man, and I said, 'I'll tell you what I'll do: I will get your farm back for you, and then you will give half of your farm to me. If I succeed, you have more than you do now, and if I fail, you have lost nothing. What do you zay?' The farmer thought about it for a while and he reluctantly agreed.

"So I went down to ze local bar, and I recruited thirty men; and for these men I get thirty automatic weapons: rifles, AK-47s, everything. Then we get thirty horses and we go riding to ze farmer's stolen ranch. I was wearing my big white hat."

He took another drink.

"We rode far into de ranch until we came across the bandits. There were many of them, but I don't know exactly how many. They were all standing there with guns. I looked at them and said, 'I work for ze farmer you have stolen dis land from; you must all leave now!' They said, 'who is going to make us?' I said, 'I am with my army of thirty men!' They said, 'What army?' I said, 'Ze army dat's right behind me!' They said, 'There is nobody behind you.' At this, I paused and turned around. It was true. There was nobody there. My army of thirty men had run away!"

At this, Ivan began to cackle with hysterical laughter, as if this was the funniest situation anyone could ever hope to encounter.

After that, he returned to his drink and never said another word about what happened with the farmer or the bandits. He didn't even have the courtesy to reveal whether or not he'd made it out of there alive.

Chapter 13

Chanka Piedra

When you reside abroad, your friends are transients. You might know them a month or a year, but the only guarantee is that they're going to move on. Before the end of my first year, Dietmar had returned to Germany, and Hiro had returned to South Korea. As a result, I fell out of the habit of going to Luz Marie's Spanish class. Instead, I spent all my time teaching.

A lot of business is done in English in Perú, so I was helping my students acquire a marketable skill. I made an effort to expand my classes beyond grammar but, after a fairly short amount of time, it became obvious that despite all my years of education I didn't have much practical knowledge. All I seemed to know were tricks for getting high scores on multiple-choice tests. That wasn't really a relevant skill for students in an impoverished district just outside of Lima.

I mostly focused on teaching my students to take control over their own ability to discern what knowledge was valuable, and how that knowledge could be acquired. I valued their insights on this topic since I was still wrestling with the problem myself.

"It's your education," I said. "Never trust it entirely to your teacher."

They thought this was an extremely funny thing to say.

On one occasion, I was just about to emphasize my sincerity when I suddenly doubled over in pain. The students gasped in shock.

"Teacher, what's the matter?"

I clenched my teeth. I realized I hadn't taught them the vocabulary to explain my problem, so I just pointed at my side.

"Pain," I said, "here." I rubbed my stomach.

"You need to drink some tea," somebody said.

What was this fascination for drinking tea?

"I tried that," I said. "I threw it up."

"It's an Inca remedy," they insisted. "You need to drink a tea called *chanka piedra*."

"Breaking stones?" I asked, loosely translating the phrase. My language comprehension was improving daily.

"Um-hmm," they replied, nodding enthusiastically.

The pain started to ebb as it sometimes did. I felt fortunate that I wouldn't have to crawl into the fetal position and cry in front of them.

I finished up class without further incident and went to talk to Luz Marie. The agony problem seemed increasingly to be something I must address.

"Have you ever heard of a tea called *chanka piedra*?" I asked Luz Marie, who was sitting at her desk eating her lunch. Her lunch consisted of a green salad and a hard-boiled egg. "One of my students mentioned it."

"Oh, that's a great idea," she said. "You should be drinking that." She set down her lunch then grabbed me by the elbow and started leading me out of the school. "There's a market nearby that might have some."

"Uh . . ." I said, but she was an irresistible force sometimes.

We were marching along at a rapid pace when she suddenly stopped in her tracks.

"Wait a minute: why did the subject even come up?"

"I doubled over in class in agony," I admitted.

Luz Marie stomped her foot. "That's it," she said. "I'm taking you to my brother the doctor." With that, she grabbed my elbow again and guided me to the market.

Many markets in Perú consist of stall after stall of wizened old ladies in front of tables overflowing with produce and the like. We stopped at a table.

"*Chanka piedra*?" Luz Marie asked.

The woman presented a plastic bag filled with leaves.

"One sol."

I paid, and we returned to the school. Luz Marie dumped the leaves into some boiling water. The water turned a sickish brown.

"Drink it."

"Can I put any sugar in it or anything?"

"No, drink it!"

I lifted the glass of nasty brownish tea to my lips. I took a drink. The flavor was bitter and brackish. It tasted like the soiled water you'd get out of the middle of the world's most horrific, churned-up peat bog. I imagined that the water had been stained with the back ends of tadpoles and tree roots that had been soaking until softened into mush.

I resisted my gag reflex and managed to swallow.

"All of it!"

I sighed and collected myself before I tried drinking again. But as I lifted the cup to my lips, I noticed something. The constant tightness I had been feeling in my side had eased. For the first time I realized I had been living in chronic pain, a steady ache, more nuisance than agony. It was glorious to have it go away. The tea had reduced it!

"Hey, I feel better," I said.

Luz Marie nodded wisely. She loved to nod wisely.

I drank some more.

"You should be drinking four or five pitchers of that a day. It will clean you out."

I looked at the hand-packaged plastic bag of leaves with new respect. It must have been the same thing they'd tried to give me in Ancon. My cultural prejudices had kept me from even giving the local remedy a chance. The stuff was effective. I hoped I'd learned to be more open to the next positive piece of advice that might come along.

"I'm still taking you to my brother the doctor," Luz Marie said.

I acquiesced. I was trying to give up control of my own destiny. There was much to be learned by submitting to the random eccentricities and brilliant ideas of strangers.

Chapter 14

We'll Just Go up and Get It

Luz Marie's doctor brother squinted at me through a pair of thick-rimmed eyeglasses. He was shuffling through a major stack of X-rays and readouts that he'd had me gather up and bring to the consultation.

Gathering up the papers had been an excursion in itself. In Perú, you go to a doctor for a consultation, and they give you a shopping list of tests that you need. However, you can't have these tests performed at the doctor's office because they don't have the hardware. Instead, you go to independent clinics.

Although this is inconvenient, the end result is that you have competition between independent clinics, who try to keep the prices down, as opposed to the hospital charging whatever it wants for the procedures, as they do in the US. My big stack of papers and X-rays had cost me a little bit of time, but in terms of cash, the whole thing had been less than $100. Included in the stack of papers was an awesome picture of the inner workings of my torso, which I had gotten by drinking a chalky mixture and then standing behind what looked like a magnet the size of a refrigerator.

The doctor was peering at this image now and shaking his head, saying, "Tsk, tsk, tsk," in that horrible, casual way doctors use to imply you'll be dead before they can get their full fee out of you.

"You see this," he said, pointing at some random blotches on the picture.

"Yes."

He rubbed his chin and nodded at me as if we'd just shared some sort of grand revelation. He kept nodding and staring at me until I had to remind him that I hadn't gone to school to study anything useful like medicine.

"What is it?" I asked, finally.

"Kidney stones."

"Ahhh . . ."

Well, that explained the pain, anyway. I'd always heard that kidney stones were pretty darn painful.

The doctor proceeded to make a bunch of buzzing and whistling sounds like R2-D2. After a moment, I realized that each whistle indicated the position of a stone. He was also tapping away on the X-ray with his pen. I might have been in consultation with a woodpecker.

"Well," I asked, "what are we going to do?"

"I'll give you a prescription," he said. "But if that doesn't work, we'll take them out."

"Take them out?" My Spanish had gotten better, but I could still be left behind if I didn't concentrate.

He nodded and, by way of demonstration, put the tip of his pen on the groin area of my X-ray.

"Take them out," he said again. Then he made a whistling sound as he thrust his pen up through the groin area on the image.

I blanched. "Why don't we just assume those pills are going to work?"

Chapter 15

Basketball in the Olives

The other American teacher, Kyle, had talked me into a weekly game of basketball. The only problem was that this meant going all the way back to Los Olivos on weekends. Still, it was worth it — for the game. Between the *chanka piedra* and the medication from the doctor, I could keep my kidney stones under control enough to play.

I was waiting at the bus stop where Ricardo Palma crosses the Via Expresa for a guy we'd met who called himself Snoop. I'd been spending more time hanging out in the "tourist" places. As a result, I'd been meeting new people. Most of them were transient characters in the middle of their own aimless journeys, like me.

The individuals you befriend abroad are different than the ones you'd hang out with back in your home country. You're constantly on the lookout for travelers who share your language or have a common background. Because such people are in short supply, you can't afford to maintain any habitual prejudices.

The result is that you stop dismissing people for their religion, political views, or the sports team they follow. You quit being concerned about how associating with a given person is going to reflect on you, or the status it might cost you in your well-worn social circle. In short, you're forced by circumstances to adopt a more tolerant attitude. The consequence is that you open up to the possibility of new ideas, and you end up forging rewarding friendships you never would have experienced otherwise.

I wasn't expecting Snoop to be on time. The buses buzzed by furiously, sending up plumes of smoke, dust, and all manner of black pollution.

Snoop was fun-loving and about my age, but I was still trying to get a read on him. Even when living abroad, you still must exercise caution and evaluate the people you meet. Between the bus ride and the actual game, I figured I'd learn everything I needed to know about Snoop before the day was done.

"Hey, man!" said a happy voice behind me: Snoop had arrived.

He looked a bit worse for wear, as if his teeth were trying to crawl off his bearded face. He wore a white T-shirt and blue jeans with a pink belt. He was very proud of his pink belt.

"Hey, dude, what's wrong?" I asked.

Snoop shook his head, wide-eyed. "Man, I tell ya, I was out drinking until six in the morning. I've had two hours of sleep."

"Uh-oh."

"Yeah, but it's nothing. Back when I was living in Nicaragua, I used to get up at like, four in the morning every day."

The thing about Snoop was that he was always dropping casual weird nuggets like that, expecting you to ask, "What? Could you explain?" But I had already caught on to his sneaky tricks, so I just nodded as if I understood everything, thus stealing all the mystery. This effect was compounded when the next person went ahead and said, "What? Could you explain?"

The bus came.

"This is it!" I said.

"What, we're taking a bus?"

"Heck, yeah!"

"Seriously? I'm more of a taxi man."

"Don't be crazy, we're going to save two dollars doing this, and the ride is only like an hour longer."

"Wha . . ."

But I was fed up with his fussing; I pushed him aboard.

"Come on! I thought you were a freedom fighter in Costa Rica? I thought you gun-fought for money in Thailand?"

"It was Indonesia . . ."

"Same difference."

The bus swallowed us up and roared off.

Snoop started telling me a story. His stories were always rapid-fire and incoherent:

"So I was taking a tour group through Mexico when this police officer tried to pull me over. He came up beside me and started screaming, 'Pull over, pull over, pull over!' and I just looked at him and shook my head no. Then he started swerving at me with his dinky motorcycle, and all the Asians and Germans and Americans in my little tour bus started freaking out, so I pulled over. But I wasn't done yet. As soon as the cop started walking up to me, I grabbed somebody's camera and took his picture. Then I grabbed his name plaque, and I wrote down his name. And once I had all that information, the guy was afraid to do anything to me, so he let us go! It's a little-known fact, but those are the steps you take to avoid trouble in Mexico."

"Well, obviously . . ." I said, and stared off into the distance.

"I'm like one step from being a grand master in chess, you know," Snoop continued.

"Yeah, I could tell."

We stood swaying in silence.

The bus went through the center of Lima and then clipped along down the Panamericana Sur. Snoop didn't like the look of it.

"Wow, man, where are you taking me?"

"Basketball."

The bus rumbled. Other, smaller cars bounced off it. Snoop started to freak out.

"When we go back, we're taking a taxi. This is crazy."

"Really?" I said. "You think so?"

He snorted.

"I take this ride every day."

"Yeah? You're crazy."

The bus finally arrived. We got out at the Los Olivos underpass and made our way through the gray tunnel in the direction of the basketball court.

I could see evidence of Snoop's hangover flashing across his face in waves. We walked along a brick wall and finally stopped at a small metal door. We had to stoop to enter. Inside was a large soccer field with a small basketball court nestled in the back. A wall extended around three sides of the complex. The fourth side terminated in a large hill covered in loose stones. The basketball court itself was white concrete. The whole complex was built between about fifty high-voltage electric towers that snapped and crackled maliciously.

"You *play* under those?"

"Sure, dude!"

"You're going to get cancer!"

"Naw, that's never been proven . . . "

"Sure it has —"

But I cut him off as everybody came over to say hello.

"Hey! This is my friend, Snoop. Hi, how are you doing?"

The basketball players were happy to see us. They were taking a class at the school, and none of them were very good. Basketball was a game they associated with the US, so they figured that since I was a white guy, I must be really awesome at it. They were also impressed by the fact that I could jump up and actually touch the backboard.

When I did a layup, they stopped and applauded.

The truth is, I'd never liked basketball all that much back in the US, but I found the game is a lot more fun when you're the tallest guy on the court and the only one who can dribble.

We started. Snoop couldn't make a shot. His legs were a little wobbly, and he had a hard time changing direction; but his spirits were high, and the Peruvians seemed happy to have him there. Then, miraculously, in the middle of the game, he made a ridiculous steal, sprinted down the court, and did a fantastic one-handed floater that slipped through the hoop with a swishing sound, despite the fact that there was no net. Snoop didn't even watch the ball go in; he just nodded once and came trotting back to the other end of the court.

It was an awesome display. I felt happy for Snoop; it was nice to see that guy in the midst of a fleeting instant of perfection, since I was under the distinct impression that those moments were few.

"I think I need to take a break," Snoop said as he approached me.

With that, he found a foot-wide piece of shade on the concrete and lay down to sleep for an hour and a half. I continued to play.

"What's wrong with your friend?" everybody asked.

"He's tired."

"Oh."

At the end of the day, we took a taxi back to Miraflores.

"Thanks, man, that was awesome. You going out tonight?"

"What else is there to do?"

"Great! I'll see you later then."

Snoop seemed OK. No more problems than average, anyway.

Chapter 16

A Four-Dollar Cure

Shortly after my visit to the doctor, I awoke in the middle of the night with the same terrible pain that had become an integral part of my life. I lay stretched out on my bed in the simple room I had come to call home. Residual light filtered in through the street, and the long shadows seemed especially ominous as the sweat began to bead on my brow.

The dull ache might be nothing more than a nuisance but for the fact that I knew it would slowly and inevitably grow in strength over a period of about ten hours. I sat up and uselessly dug my fist into my abdomen. I pushed as hard as I could, but I couldn't dislodge the pain.

When you have kidney stones, there are two events that can cause you agony. One is when the stone forms and fails to drop out of the kidney itself. The second is the pain of the stone passing to your bladder and then through your urethra. My pain was of the first variety. I was lucky in that when my stones actually dropped, they were small enough to pass without too much issue. But during that formative period, it was simply impossible to urinate.

Imagine experiencing the strongest, most urgent need to urinate you've ever felt in your life and simply not being able to relieve yourself. Add to that a dull ache steadily growing in intensity in the center of your torso, and you have an idea what kidney stones are like.

The first hour or so wasn't too bad. I could shift positions and distract myself into thinking that the pain had momentarily eased.

By the third hour, however, I had broken into a full sweat. The pain steadily grew, and I found myself doubling over, standing, sitting, and curling up into a fetal position, seeking relief. The whole routine was like some intense and sadistic form of yoga.

All the while, I drank my *chanka piedra*. The acrid flavor seemed to burn more and more as I struggled to swallow gallons of the stuff. The tea eased the pain somewhat, but also increased my need to urinate. Since urination wasn't possible, *chanka piedra* wasn't an ideal palliative.

The hours dragged on.

There's nothing like intense pain to make you realize you're not as tough as you thought. I would have answered any question put to me in order to end the agony. I would have given up every person, nation, and institution I ever held dear. Nobody's tough enough to withstand such pain.

It started as a pinprick and became a fiery, swirling void in the center of my being.

The pain was everything.

It increased and increased and increased in intensity until . . .

It stopped!

The release was instant. There was no sound or sensation other than the simple feeling that the blockage had been removed. I shuffled off to the bathroom and relieved myself of what seemed like a couple gallons of processed *chanka piedra*.

Finally free of the shackles of torture, I threw myself into bed.

Fighting that stone had exhausted me, and I fell instantly to sleep, although I was somewhat perturbed by a flashing image of the doctor digging into my kidneys with a rusty coat hanger, and using the only open avenue available to get there.

The next evening, Marisol gave me a stern look. "We're sick of hearing you battle those stones," she said.

I looked at her. I was sick of fighting them myself, but I didn't know what she could do about it. What I didn't know then was that she had a plan.

She grabbed me by the arm and led me into the kitchen. There, a whole array of implements lay on the table. It looked like a cross between a herbal remedy shop and the laboratory of a deranged botanist.

"Sit down," she barked.

I sat.

From my new vantage point, I saw she had some water boiling. I thought of the emergency birth scenes of a thousand daytime movies where a desperate, untrained husband or passerby begins screaming for hot water.

Hot water cures everything.

Marisol put a cup in front of me. It appeared to be a normal coffee cup. She lifted a bottle of olive oil and poured it into the cup.

The viscous liquid oozed like sludge and sat there quivering in anticipation.

"What do I do with that?" I asked.

"Drink it."

"All of it?"

"The whole cup!"

"What's the hot water for?"

"You'll find out in a moment."

I sighed, but there was no way to resist Marisol.

I put the cup to my lips. With a quick motion, I tilted my head and dumped the olive oil into my mouth. It flowed with agonizing slowness down my throat. I sucked the thick liquid down with every ounce of strength I had in me, coming up for breath briefly, only to dive into the cup once again.

"All of it!" Marisol urged.

A thousand years of my drinking gallons of straight olive oil passed in a terrible second. I went into the challenge not really knowing what a mouthful of olive oil tasted like, and I was trying to finish before the actual knowledge of that taste managed to make its way from my tongue to my brain. The olive oil was not helping me, however. The stuff seemed to sprout octopus arms and cling tenaciously to my mouth and throat as I attempted to swallow. The mischievous, reaching tendrils found the soft path in my esophagus that causes a gag reflex and started tap dancing.

I came up for breath once again.

"All!" Marisol responded.

I looked into the cup; there was just a mouthful left in the bottom.

"I can't."

"All!" Marisol insisted.

About to lift the cup to my mouth and try again, I remembered that I was an adult and didn't need to do things I didn't want to do. "No, I'm not drinking any more. That's all I can take," I said, and pushed the cup aside.

Marisol seemed to weigh whether or not she should press the issue. After a moment, she gave up, reaching instead for the hot water. She squeezed a couple of lemons into the water and handed me a glass.

"Now drink this."

"What's this for?"

"This is to wash the olive oil out of your mouth and throat."

I smacked my lips and realized the necessity of a cleansing. I lifted the hot water/lemon mix and rinsed out my mouth and throat.

"What's next?" I said.

"Now you must sit up all night and not throw up."

Fortunately, I'd experienced a lot of nights where my whole objective was to sit up straight and not throw up, so I wasn't too worried about that. Still, I had questions:

"What's going to happen in the morning?"

"In the morning, the stones will come out." To emphasize this, she made a "pbbbthhh" sound.

I shrugged and shuffled off to the chair she'd set up in my room.

That fiendish glob of olive oil was not at all content to be entrapped in the depths of my belly, and immediately I could feel the liquid attempt to climb back out the door through which it had entered. But I resisted the effort, and halfway through the night the olive oil and I reached an uneasy truce. I even slept a little bit.

In the morning, I felt like the leftover refuse from a mud spa. However, when I went to urinate, I heard the machine-gun sound of kidney stones striking porcelain.

"Well, I'll be . . ." I muttered.

A complete and total cure.

I never had problems with kidney stones again.

It was a relief to know that those horrible stones, at least, weren't going to be what did me in. It looked as if I'd need to find something else to do the job.

Chapter 17

The Pleasure of Being Robbed

Sometimes I'd get up in the morning and go down to the nearest bodega for breakfast. In the early hours of the day, there was always a pleasant moisture in the air, and the traffic on the side streets was minimal. The bodega was a tiny business about the size of a single car garage. The walls were lined with boxes of milk, cookies, and other common pantry items. They even had eggs behind the counter. There was also a single chair and a small table. Their breakfast special consisted of an egg inside a roll of bread for one sol. Coffee was an additional sol.

I'd discovered early that the side street bodegas of Lima had the best coffee. They bring you a pot of boiling water and a small flask of something called "essence of coffee." You then mix the essence and the hot water in a cup to your liking.

The coffee and the roll lured me into random contemplations, and when I finally got around to looking up at the clock, I was surprised to notice I was running late. I leaped to my feet, paid my S/. 2, and ran outside to flag down the first *combi* that appeared.

The *combi* was tightly packed. I hadn't been expecting to get a seat, but on this *combi* even the standing room was body-to-body. As the vehicle accelerated away, passengers groaned in protest as the crowd of humanity lurched forward and backward in unison.

Oblivious to the overloading of the bus, its driver continued to stop for every pedestrian who raised an arm, despite the protests of the cramped passengers onboard. Soon people had to scream, yell, and fight just to get off at their stops.

A heavyset man dropped a bunch of coins at my feet. Despite the chaos, he got down on his hands and knees to pick up his coins, pulling at my feet and pushing them aside in pursuit of his lost change.

I took pity on the fellow, assuming that the coins he had dropped represented a vast sum of money to him. However, I thought it odd how much attention he paid to pushing my feet around. In the midst of all the confusion, I was trying to signal the doorman that I wanted to disembark. He gave me a blank stare as the bus slowed, and I pushed my way to the door.

When I got off the bus, I kept thinking about the heavyset man on his hands and knees. "That was odd," I said to myself. "It was almost like . . . a distraction!"

The realization sent a chill down my spine as I suddenly understood the truth of what had happened. Half in panic, I reached down to the zip-up pocket that held my wallet, only to find the familiar leather bulge missing.

The bus drove off into the distance, leaving me helpless and sputtering in the street.

I watched it go in a haze of red. I was very, very angry.

As if sensing my fury, the crowd parted around me as I stomped along toward the school. I still had some loose change, so I stopped at a call center and canceled the credit card I'd also had in my wallet before entering through the gate. Luz Marie was there to meet me at the door.

"What's wrong?" She'd caught a glimpse of the storm cloud forming over my head and was concerned.

I told her the story. She was sympathetic. "It happens to everyone who lives in Lima eventually."

"Yes, but I should have realized what was going on. That's the oldest trick in the book."

"Don't be too hard on yourself," she continued. "After all, street thieves are professionals. How much did you lose?"

"About fifty US dollars."

She hissed as if she considered this to be an enormous sum which I shouldn't have been carrying around town in the first place.

"Well, today is payday, so at least you'll have something to get you home."

I'd forgotten about that. I'd just finished up my first month of teaching, and it was time to begin the arduous process of getting paid. I was only in Perú on a tourist visa, so technically it wasn't legal for me to work. But that wasn't a problem because everybody worked in Perú without the proper documentation. That was the local norm, and it is commonly said that you should follow the local norm when you are a guest in a country. I didn't wish to be accused of being ethnocentric. Perú is populated with expat backpackers who came to the land of the Incas and decided to stay since everyone thought them "professional teachers" due to their status as native speakers of English.

"What do I need to do to get paid?" I asked Luz Marie.

"Somebody must give you a document called *Recibos por Honorarios*. It's sort of an official receipt that shows you've accepted money."

"Won't those people have to pay taxes on that money?"

"You only pay taxes if you receive more than S/. 1,100 per *Recibo*. So you can avoid taxes by receiving your payments in smaller amounts."

That made zero sense to me, but I decided not to question the local tax code because my own government often did things I found totally incomprehensible.

Luz Marie rounded up somebody willing to give me a couple *Recibos*, and I went up to the pay window, where I received a sweaty wad of bills that amounted to around S/. 1,500, which was the equivalent of just under 500 dollars.

I zipped the money into a hidden inner pocket of my jacket.

The day passed without incident, although I was a little testier with my students than was fair. My irritation over the robbery continued to linger.

The prospect of riding the evening bus home with all my wages in cash concerned me, but I was lucky. There were few passengers, and the ones that did climb aboard took one look at me and steered clear.

I got off the bus for the final leg of my journey still bristling at the slightest provocation. As I made my way along my street, two young men came sprinting around a corner in front of me. I watched as the bigger of the two men threw the smaller one against a wall and started digging in his backpack.

All at once I realized I was witnessing a robbery!

In a split second, I decided I wasn't going to allow this to happen. In the majority of situations, you're probably better off not getting involved. After all, the whole thing might be a con designed to sucker you in. But I had too much residual rage lingering in me to witness a robbery and do nothing.

I puffed up and sprinted over to the altercation.

"What's going on?" I roared.

The bigger kid who was digging in the backpack turned whiter than a sheet and froze.

The other kid, the one who was having his backpack rifled through, looked up at me and shook his hands in a negative gesture.

"Everything is OK," he said.

"You're OK?"

He nodded.

I relaxed and passed them by. It was only about a block later that I realized the two of them were probably brothers who were just horsing around.

In the end, I managed get over my anger by channeling it into my workouts at the gym. You can't do anything about the sense of helplessness that overwhelms you after getting robbed, but you can work yourself to the point of exhaustion

In time my fury waned, but my extra awareness never did. You can think you've prepared yourself mentally for the prospect of having people steal from you, but until it actually happens, you're not as prepared as you think.

The lesson had cost me fifty dollars.

I've paid ten times more for lessons that didn't teach me half as much.

I was never robbed again. Overall, I've lost a lot more money to dubious fines back in the US than pickpockets I've encountered abroad. The concept of safety is relative.

Chapter 18

The English-Speaking Beggar

When I had nothing else to do I enjoyed walking through the busy streets of Miraflores and soaking up the ambiance of the city. Avenida Larco boasted a wide assortment of shops, restaurants, and cafes that were always bustling with action. Near the Ovalo de Miraflores sits a Saga Falabella, with a Ripley just off Parque Kennedy; these are Lima's two main department stores and they served as the center for the general fashion trends of the nation. Avenida Larco stretched all the way to the ocean, and about four in the evening the sidewalks became crowded with people leaving work and heading home.

One evening I found myself walking down Avenida Larco. The sun was covered by the overcast skies, and the wind carried a saltwater smell as it meandered between the bustling pedestrians of the city.

People of all shapes and sizes marched by on urgent errands. It was natural to mingle with them. Their shoulders would brush mine for an instant before they were swept off by the indomitable current of their lives. Strangers who were potential friends, enemies, or lovers went silently on their way. The great majority would never cross my path again, although there were some who seemed to spiral back with a strange and lethargic pull of inevitability.

These were like actors waiting for a cue to reveal the greater part they'd have to play.

"Excuse me," said a voice.

I looked up from my thoughts to see a Caucasian face. He was slight of build, tall, and had an inviting, innocent grin.

"Do you speak English?" he said, and I thought I detected a British accent. I presumed he was not Peruvian, perhaps an Englishman on vacation.

"Yes," I replied.

"Oh, what a relief," he said.

People continued to pass on the street. Beautiful women offered shy smiles behind dark hair. All at once, I began to feel agitated that this strange fellow had picked me out from the flow. It felt creepy.

"Bye," I said, moving to get around him, but he stepped in front of me.

"It's just that I've had a bit of trouble," he said. His face was still split open in an attempt at a genial expression, but now there seemed something sinister about him. "All of my luggage was stolen; what a nightmare."

I didn't want to hear more, but I couldn't extract myself gracefully.

"Isn't there anyone you can call?"

"I don't have any money."

So there it was.

At first I considered forcing my way around him, but then I thought back to all the people who had helped me while I was in Perú. Perhaps this was a way to reward the faith they had shown with their generous assistance.

After my last robbery, I'd gotten into the habit of never leaving the house with much money. I reached into my pocket and extracted a bill. When I brought it to the light, I was relieved to see it was only a S/. 10 note.

"This is all I have," I said, offering it to the man. He snatched the paper from my hand, and I maneuvered around him back into the flow of foot traffic, back on my way.

"Thank you," he said, "perhaps you can give me your contact information so I can repay you?"

"That's OK," I said, not looking back, "it's a gift."

I continued along, trying to recuperate the sense of ease I'd been falling into before the interruption, but it was lost to me.

*

A few days later, I was again making my way down Avenida Larco, this time at night. The light from the streetlamps created pools of utter blackness that stretched like fingers into the street. A voice came out of the darkness, causing me to jump.

I looked around for the source of the voice and saw a man on the other side of the street.

"Excuse me," the man said, waving as if we were old friends. "Excuse me!"

Something about him did look familiar. I scoured my memory as I watched him attempt to cross the heavily trafficked street. He was having a hard time as vehicle after vehicle barred his way. Before he managed to cross, I recognized him as the same man I'd given the S/. 10 note to some time before.

All at once, I understood with certainty that this guy was a con artist. I'd come to suspect it after my first encounter with him, but the nights of reflection had left me better prepared for the second interaction.

"Are you coming to repay me my S/. 10?" I said.

At this, the man stopped in his tracks. The friendly smile dropped from his face, and his features underwent a startling transformation. Gone was the warmth that had appeared in his eyes, to be replaced by a rodent-like suspicion. I realized with a start that this uglier aspect was his true appearance. The understanding sent a shiver down my spine.

He instantly ceased his effort to cross the street and jumped back to the curb to continue on his way in the opposite direction.

"What about my S/. 10?" I called after him. "You owe me S/. 10!" I was suddenly angry. Angry that someone had taken advantage of my charitable impulse.

I considered what I could have done with that S/. 10. There are those in Lima whose lives would have been noticeably improved by obtaining such a trifling sum. Yet there I was, inclined to provide charity to a light-skinned man mainly because he spoke the same language I did.

The thought left me sick to my stomach.

I turned and continued on my way, careful to glance behind me in case I should see this mysterious stranger approaching with more sinister intent. But he'd scurried off out of sight.

*

I crossed paths with the English-speaking beggar a few more times over the next few months. I couldn't help but conjecture as to his story. Perhaps he had escaped something back in his home nation and had come to reside in Perú to avoid persecution. He always approached me with a smile, only to have the expression drop away when I revealed I'd lent him S/. 10 on a previous meeting. The moment I said that, something like disgust or panic would enter his eyes, and he'd make haste up the road or across the street.

I saw him four or five times, and after every meeting I felt a little more emboldened. Eventually, I'd scream out, "You owe me S/. 10," even before he'd had a chance to hail me. On these occasions he'd retreat as if wounded, and I realized that to an outside observer I must have looked like the irrational aggressor.

This strange interplay continued for quite some time; and although we crossed paths with some frequency, the repeated exchanges didn't seem to help his ability to remember me. He always approached like a friend, then scurried away like a bruised and battered puppy when I snapped at him.

Normally I saw him on the street, where I could get away if necessary, but on the last occasion I met him I was sitting in a small *chifa* restaurant on Calle Tarata.

My plate of pineapple chicken and rice still hadn't arrived when he appeared, so I couldn't get up and leave as my instincts urged. Instead, I hardened my expression and hoped a last shred of decency would stop him from taking a seat.

I'd developed a deeply-rooted dislike for the English-speaking beggar, mainly because I saw no excuse for his behavior. He was fluent in a foreign language, after all, and that skill alone should have been enough for him to find employment if he wanted to work. Sure, teaching didn't pay much, but it paid enough so that you didn't have to con people.

As he stood in the doorway, his eyes met mine; that familiar, false, cynical smile spread across his features.

"Hello," he said. "Do you speak English?"

His eyes were wide, and his face unguarded as he stepped toward me.

"You know I do," I snapped.

He stopped.

"Why do you keep approaching me?" I said. "I gave you S/. 10 two months ago when we crossed paths on Larco. Did you forget?"

He sat down and looked away. As always when I pressed him, he ignored me. This time, the action was overt and made me angry. "Are you going to buy me lunch today? I bought you lunch back then, it seems."

His head snapped around, and this time the visage of the meek beggar was completely absent. In its place was the scowl of a predator.

"I ain't got a dime, kid!" he said, without any trace of a British accent.

The transformation was unnerving. I was young and strong, but I didn't know what his limits were. Crazy people do crazy things, it's best not to engage them.

The silence lingered, broken only by the clinking of jostled plates.

He didn't look at me again.

I waited for my food, took it, and left.

I didn't see him after that, not in a restaurant, not on the street, not anywhere. After a while, the agitation I'd felt from the anticipation of running into him began to ease.

But he never left my thoughts entirely.

I couldn't help but wonder if that was how I was going to end up, if I didn't start making more serious plans for the future.

Chapter 19

Kill or Cure

I finally came to believe I had a pretty good grasp on things in Perú. My Spanish had gotten pretty solid, I had developed a good feel for the culture, and I'd learned to navigate the incomprehensible bus system, which allowed me to get virtually anywhere in Lima for one nuevo sol.

Some places I visited on occasion made me a bit nervous, since they were dangerous, but as long as you left those districts before dark there usually weren't any issues. After a while, it all became routine, and soon the whole focus of my life became the spirited basketball games the school set up on the weekends.

Players included a bunch of Peruvians who were regulars, but since basketball is not one of the major sports in Perú, they persisted in their misconception that I was actually competent at the game. Over time, I developed a lot of affection for the players. They were very accepting of me. They each learned

123

my name and greeted me when I arrived, although a couple of them seemed to have trouble understanding my Spanish.

On Saturday mornings I would wake up, get dressed in my ragged shorts and shoes, eat a packet of crackers, and hike out to the bus stop. I always brought a ball and a couple jugs of water in my duffel bag. The Saturday bus ride was always less hectic than the work week trips, and I could reflect and observe the city during the trip. When I finally arrived in Los Olivos, I would hike out to the court and await the arrival of the players.

The girls arrived first and played a couple all-girl games as the boys trickled in. As the boys began to arrive, they'd be added to the rosters, with players rotating in and out as they got tired. These early games were more teaching sessions than actual contests,because many of the participants didn't know the rules. Those games were delightful, though, as the players laughed and chased loose balls rolling and bouncing out of bounds. Occasionally you'd see a student get frustrated and, rather than catch the ball with his hands, he'd do a miraculous soccer flip with his feet which sent the ball on a perfect arc to land gently in the cradle of his arms.

The sight helped me remember that basketball was as foreign to them as the Spanish language was to me.

After a while, we'd play a couple more informal games, in which each team would have both boys and girls. One or two of the girls were very good, so I'd constantly feed them the ball and tell them to shoot. Others were just learning; these tended to dribble the ball so high that it would bounce over their heads and roll out of bounds.

Everyone had a good sense of humor about such errors, and the game carried on with no hard feelings. The emphasis was on fun, a nice contrast from the ultra-competitive sporting activities I'd played back in the States.

As the tallest person on the court, I usually just camped out under the basket, waiting for a rebound, then launched the ball to the other end in a full court pass. The guys who were on my team quickly became trained to sprint to the other end of the court as soon as someone took a shot.

After an hour or so of playing with the girls, we'd make new teams with just the boys.

For the most part the games stayed pretty civilized, but you can't play a huge amount of basketball without twisting an ankle sooner or later.

I was in the midst of a spirited scuffle for a rebound when I jumped and landed awkwardly to an audible "pop!" as something dislocated itself in my foot. The school provided a trainer who always prowled the sidelines in a smart white sweat suit. At the sight of my distress, he ran over and worked painfully on my ankle for a few minutes. Eventually he jammed hard on the bottom of my heel and something snapped back into place.

Like a fool, I kept playing for the next hour or so, hobbling back and forth until the swelling became so bad they tapped me on the shoulder and made me go home. The swelling was exacerbated by the sedentary bus ride back to Miraflores, and when I got to my house I was limping in a fashion that I knew I couldn't hide from Marisol.

The thought of Marisol observing my distress was quite scary, because I knew she would take it upon herself to "cure" me.

By the time the bus reached Miraflores, I was hungry and nauseated all at the same time. My plan had been to buy a rotisserie quarter chicken at Wong's and some ibuprofen at the pharmacy, then slip into my bed, hopefully unnoticed. Halfway home, I realized that I was swooning too much to even contemplate making detours from the most direct line between the bus stop and my waiting mattress. Nevertheless, I had hunger pangs. Reluctantly, I picked up my phone.

"Hi," I said, ringing up Marisol's daughter, Jocelyn. "Could you do me a favor? Could you pick me up some ibuprofen and a quarter chicken? I'll pay you back when I get home. Oh, and don't tell your mom."

Over the months, I'd developed a pretty good relationship with Jocelyn, mainly because I'd had a talk with a couple of security guards who were in the habit of cat-calling her as she came home from school. I was surprised when she came to me for help, but her story filled me with so much anger that I stomped out of the house and made the two guys apologize and promise never to do it again.

"We didn't do anything," they claimed.

"Are you calling her a liar?" I asked with crazy eyes.

My glare shut them up. It's amazing how the strength comes to you when you're in the right.

The importance of a mother is beyond argument, but young girls also need a dad around to keep the wolves at bay. I wasn't a dad exactly, but that didn't mean I'd let the wolves have a free pass.

Despite this level of trust, you couldn't ask somebody to sneak you ibuprofen and chicken without expecting to answer a few questions.

"What happened?" Jocelyn asked through the static of the poor phone connection.

"I sprained my ankle," I explained. "I just want to eat and go to bed."

Jocelyn voiced an unwarranted degree of worry that I tried to quell. One of the most touching and admirable characteristics of the Peruvian people is how genuinely concerned they become for those sick or injured. Their desire to smother you with love and attention truly is a beautiful quality, but it sometimes clashes with the American philosophy of wanting to be solitary so that you can quietly go off into the wilderness to die. Navigating the different cultural responses to various scenarios is half the fun of living abroad. Eventually I calmed her down and hung up.

The bus stopped, and I struggled to my feet. Every step was a searing agony. The journey seemed to stretch on for decades. Sustaining me were thoughts of my soft bed, the quiet of my room, and the taste of

the quarter chicken that would (hopefully) be awaiting me.

I reached the door to the house, turned my key,
and chaos immediately ensued.

"Oh my god! What have you done to yourself? I
can't believe this has happened! Are you OK?" Marisol
had found out the truth! I turned an icy glare on Jocelyn, who apologetically held up a plastic bag containing a quarter chicken. Well, at least there was that.

"Did you get the ibuprofen?" I asked, paying her
for the chicken.

"Ibuprofen!" exclaimed my host mother in disgust. She had gathered up a couple of her friends from
the neighborhood to support her. "Who ever heard of
treating a sprained ankle with ibuprofen? Crazy American! I suppose you were going to put ice on it, too?"

The conglomeration of women began laughing.

"Actually, I was," I responded.

After a collective gasp of horror, they hustled me
into the living room and sat me down. Here, waiting
for me like some primitive torture device, sat a caul-
dron of steaming water with strange herbs floating in
it.

"Sit down!" they commanded.

I sat.

"Put your foot in there."

"But it's boiling hot!"

"No, it's not," Marisol said. She splashed her
hand in the water to show me how harmless it was.
"See, it won't hurt you."

"There's a big difference between splashing your hand in boiling water and submerging it —"

They whipped off my shoe and plunged my foot into the basin.

"GHHAAAHHH!"

"Oh, quit being such a baby." Marisol splashed her hand a few more times to demonstrate how silly I was. "See, it's not hot at all!"

I clenched my teeth and endured the herb-infused hot water for a few minutes.

My foot turned as red as a lobster.

As if triggered by the agony, I remembered a stash of ibuprofen that I'd hidden in my room from my last Sunday-morning headache. I stumbled to my feet.

"Where are you going?"

"Bathroom," I lied. I grabbed my quarter chicken on the way.

Once I'd crawled into my room and locked the door, I stood panting, trapped between fear and hilarity.

Marisol aspired to "put me right." But I wished she'd let me have a say in the matter.

I found the plastic packet with the little orange pills and took several of them eagerly. Within ten minutes, the swelling was down, and the pain had almost gone away. I stepped out of my room a little while later.

"You see," Marisol said, "the treatment worked!"

I decided not to argue with her, thanked her graciously, and went to bed. The whole escapade was another reminder of how different my cultural background was from hers. They treated sprained ankles with boiling water and herbs; I treated them with medication and ice. The world was beautiful and diverse. Secretly, we all think that those with preferred alternatives to our tried and true methods are crazy. Scientific exploration of effectiveness rarely enters the evaluation. Even aware of my shortcomings, I was still subject to them.

However, a strange thing happened that next weekend at basketball. I arrived and took off my socks and shoes to show the massive bruise extending from above my ankle to my toes.

"Wow," said the trainer who had worked on the injury the previous week. "That's worse than I thought."

I nodded as he continued his examination.

"So," he said, flashing a grin, "how did you treat it? Ice and ibuprofen?"

I couldn't tell if he was teasing me, so I simply shrugged and got ready to play.

Chapter 20

Spanish Mistakes

Jorge Chavez international airport is rather small compared to installations you might find in similar sized metropolitan areas. It's located in Callao, just a few miles from the historic center of Lima. The concourse is about the length of a city block with towering floor to ceiling windows facing the parking lot. As airports go it's inviting enough — sufficiently sized to provide service to the major cities of the world, but not so overwhelming as to make navigation complicated. For many travelers to Perú, the airport was the only sliver of Lima they ever saw. Most guidebooks recommend going straight to Cusco, so it was common for tourists to book connecting flights leaving shortly after touchdown in Lima without scheduling any time to see the City of Kings.

Passengers from international flights arrive through customs at the south end of the building, and a large crowd customarily gathers to await friends and relatives emerging from sliding glass doors. The ladies take this occasion very seriously, and dress in stunning ensembles fit for a night on the town. I looked forward to going to the airport simply so I could observe the crowd.

On this occasion, I was awaiting my friend Grady, who had developed a curiosity about Lima based on all the stories I'd been sharing with him.

The doors in the far wall slid open, and on the heels of a crowd of strangers, my friend emerged. He was a touch over six feet tall with an athletic build and a short-cropped, military haircut. His dark complexion was a good match with the local population, and he had a day's worth of stubble on his face probably due to the extensive length of his journey. He wore jeans and a black jacket.

I waved to him and he smiled as he pushed through the crowd in my direction.

"You've lost weight," Grady said, extending his hand. I took it and then pulled him in for a hug.

"Thanks, let's go find a taxi."

We made our way outside, avoiding the first dozen or so drivers who stood around their cabs aggressively looking for passengers. I made my way to a taxi that had just unloaded his fare and haggled for a moment before Grady and I piled in.

Finally settled in the taxi, Grady continued his initial thought. "No," he said, shaking his head in concern, "you've lost a lot of weight. It's as if you went through boot camp or something."

"I guess it stresses the body — uprooting to another country and learning another language and culture," I replied with a laugh. Grady took it in his stride, but clearly harbored suspicions as to the state of my health.

When it came to boot camp, Grady knew what he was talking about. He'd done a stint in the Army and was currently a high-ranking officer in the Air Force. At one point, he was one of the nation's top experts in missile-defense coverage. If he had followed the advice of our high-school guidance counselor, he wouldn't even have gone to college. Grady ended up graduating with a degree in Chemistry and minors in Mathematics, Physics, Biology, and Computer Science. He was a sharp fellow, and my closest friend from high school.

"How did you get the clearance to come down here?" I asked, aware that the military sometimes had severe restrictions as to when and where its personnel could travel.

Grady shrugged.

"I didn't tell them," he said. "It wasn't worth the paperwork."

I laughed: same old Grady.

He had contacted me a couple weeks before about coming down to see Machu Picchu. I was going on two years in Perú and finally felt comfortable enough in my adoptive country to attempt the trip, so I'd given him the green light to join me.

"Got any luggage?"

"Just this," Grady said, holding up a small bag.

"That's not much."

"Nope, and I'm not taking anything back with me. I plan on giving away all my clothing when we get to Cusco."

The taxi flew by the billboards that lined the highway and Grady attempted to read almost every one as we headed to Miraflores. My Spanish was good at this point so I was able to correct him when he stumbled. Grady was no slouch at language acquisition, and he was looking forward to the opportunity to practice his skills.

"I've been purchasing attack helicopters lately at work," he said, switching back to English to make conversation during the drive. "I have a budget you wouldn't believe."

"What does that consist of, exactly? Do you have to go out and kick the tires?"

"Naw, it's mostly boring meetings just like any other job, although something funny did happen the other day."

"What was that?"

"One of the helicopters I reviewed was rated to minus 40 degrees, and a four-star general started berating my report for not labeling that figure as Fahrenheit or Celsius."

"I suppose he was just looking for clarification."

"The label is irrelevant, Fahrenheit and Celsius are the same at minus 40 degrees." Grady started to laugh.

I laughed too, but I thought my friend had risked too much over the Fahrenheit/Celsius intersection point. Then again, Grady had the kind of precision mind that remembers numbers exactly. My mind didn't work that way. I remembered that the point existed, but I wouldn't have bet my job on my ability to recall it. I assumed Grady hadn't taken the time to double check because that would have entailed more work than simply applying a label . . . he'd probably been intentionally vague in the hope of provoking a reaction.

The taxi made its way to Miraflores without incident, and soon Grady was set up in my little room. Marisol had given me special permission to let him stay, since it was only for a few days. I had a series of activities ready for Grady, and with no shortage of glee I sprung the first one on him:

"Did you bring any formal clothing?" I asked as he made himself comfortable.

"Not really," Grady replied.

"That's OK, I don't have any either. Just grab a shirt with some buttons."

"Why?"

"Because we're going to a wedding."

*

One of Marisol's friends from Ancon had a daughter who was marrying a used-car salesman from Italy. They had met online, and he'd arrived the week before. The wedding was a whirlwind affair. I think I'd been invited just to help fill a couple of seats.

I asked Marisol about our clothing predicament, but she assured me we would look fine.

"Gringos are always dressed casually," she said. "We're used to it."

I didn't know what she meant until later that night when we showed up at the church. Indeed, everyone wore dressy clothes to the event but for Grady and me. The men wore tailored suits and did not confine themselves to the standard black you see at formal events in the United States. No, their suits covered a wide spectrum, including brown, gray, green, blue, and even white. In every case, their shoes and belts matched the color of their suits exactly.

If the wardrobe choice of the men was surprising, the vestments of the women were utterly jaw-dropping. All wore colors and designs that resembled those in an elite fashion magazine. Their athletic bodies were highlighted by shiny bronzed skin and raven black hair. "They're stunning," Grady said.

"The men or the women?" I replied.

"Both."

I looked down at myself. I'd managed a button-down shirt, and my belt was the same color as my shoes, but I was clearly outclassed. It didn't matter, however; everyone made us feel welcome. The ceremony was held in a massive cathedral and went on so long that I thought the bridesmaids might collapse. Afterward, we walked through an atrium to salute the bride and groom. I even shared a private laugh with the groom. He was as much a stranger to everyone involved in the ceremony as I was.

After the formal greeting came the mixer, where we lounged around sipping drinks and grabbing shrimp from offered trays.

"This is incredible," Grady exclaimed. "How did you manage to get us invited to this?"

"I don't know really," I replied. "Ever since I moved here, things like this just seem to happen."

Grady and I were a bit of a novelty. Curious people approached us. Grady seized the opportunity to test his Spanish fluency.

The funny thing about learning foreign languages is that whenever you make an error in word choice or pronunciation you invariably say something totally inappropriate and probably sexual in nature. No matter how careful you are to dodge this trap, you'll get caught sooner or later. My advice is to make no attempt at avoidance; just enjoy your status as the "innocent" foul-mouthed life of the party.

Two lovely girls stepped over, wearing the orange dresses of bridesmaids. It was clear they had spent a couple hours at the salon that day in preparation for the ceremony, and the results were miraculous. After the typical introductions, they asked us if we were going to Machu Picchu.

"Yes," Grady replied. "I'm very excited about it."

Or at least, that's what he meant to say. Naturally he assumed that the Spanish word for "excited" was just the English word with an "o" at the end. So what he said was, "*Estoy excitado*!" which had a meaning very different from, "I'm excited!"

The phrase caused the girls to break out into uncontainable laughter.

"What's going on?" Grady asked me.

"You just said that you are sexually aroused."

Grady blanched and started waving his hands.

"No, no," he said, and then started searching for words. He tried saying that he was embarrassed, again pronouncing the English word with a Spanish accent and putting an "o" on the end.

"*Estoy muy embarazado*," he spouted.

This only caused the ladies to cackle all the more.

"What did I do this time?" he asked me.

"You just said you were very pregnant," I replied, not able to suppress my own urge to chuckle.

"I give up," Grady said.

I felt guilty, laughing along with the others at Grady's pronunciation errors, but before the night was over, the biggest laugh would be on me.

After the mixer we headed out to a fancy restaurant, where we were seated at a long table with a white tablecloth and given menus. To save himself further embarrassment, Grady let me order for him. Looking down at the menu, I decided that the smoked trout looked appealing.

The correct phrase for smoked trout is *trucha ahumada*.

Unfortunately, when I spoke, the phrase everyone at the table heard was *chucha mojada*. I would come to learn that there is a big difference between *trucha ahumada* and *chucha mojada*.

However, my only initial indication that something was amiss was an awkward silence that spread rapidly in all directions with me as an uncomfortably obvious starting point.

"Bring me a plate of *chucha mojada*."

The words lay upon the table like a veil of shame. The waiter looked at me with a quizzical expression.

"*Perdón, señor?*" he said.

"*Chucha mojada,*" I declared again, annoyed that I was drawing so much attention.

The words provoked a few chuckles that echoed like a cricket's song. The moment dragged out with increasing awkwardness.

"Excuse me," one of the English-speaking members of the wedding party finally said. She was an attractive woman about my age. "What are you trying to order?"

I sighed in annoyance and picked up my menu. It irritated me when people claimed they couldn't understand my Spanish, which I knew to be good enough for most practical purposes like ordering a plate of smoked trout.

"This!" I declared, pointing at my selection.

"Oh, *trucha ahumada!*"

There was an abrupt release of pressure as everyone at the table sighed in comprehension and then burst into uncontrolled laughter. The waiter nodded in relief and sprinted off toward the kitchen. This unexpected jubilation irritated me.

"That's what I said, *chucha mojada!*" I replied, still not understanding what all the fuss was about.

"Um," said the English speaker, "what you're saying is different."

"It sounds the same to me," I said, doggedly pursuing the matter like a fool.

"Well, first of all, you're using a 'ch' sound instead of a 't' sound, which makes the first word you're saying sound less like the Spanish word for 'trout' and more like a fairly dirty piece of street slang."

I began to color.

"Which word am *I* saying?"

"*Chucha*," she said, her voice dropping down to a whisper.

"What's it slang for?"

Her voice dropped even more.

"Vagina," she admitted apologetically.

Now came Grady's turn to laugh.

I could only sit there and shake my head.

"But that's not the end of it," my translator continued. "In the second word of the phrase, you are using a 'mo' sound instead of an 'ah' sound."

"Let me guess, more slang?"

"No, in this case it's merely an unfortunate adjective."

"What?"

"*Mojada* . . . meaning moist."

I sat dumfounded for a moment as the terrible realization dawned on me.

"You mean," I said, "instead of 'smoked trout' I was ordering a plate of . . . 'moist vagina'?"

The girl could only nod.

Grady just about fell off his chair.

"Well, I'm glad you're enjoying yourself," I said. But there was no getting through to him: he laughed and laughed until his face turned red and tears poured down his cheeks. After a while, he calmed down enough to engage in conversation, until a casual glance in my direction got him roaring again. There were usually a dozen or so people willing to join him.

I was still hoping to lay the blame elsewhere.

"It seems kind of devious to make those two phrases sound so similar, doesn't it?" I said. The result was another roar of amusement from Grady.

I tried to remain sullen, but found that I couldn't resist the sheer joy my poor pronunciation seemed to have caused. Soon I gave up the petulant act and started laughing as well.

After a while, I turned to my translator, who had also joined in the fun, for one final thought.

"You know," I said, "you shouldn't have corrected me. It would have been amusing to see what the waiter brought back from the kitchen."

Chapter 21

Cusco's Five-Dollar Hotels

The next morning Grady and I got up and began preparations for our journey to Cusco, the next stop on our journey to Machu Picchu. We traveled light, a backpack each, and set off from Marisol's to have breakfast before hailing a cab to the airport. We checked in with no difficulty, and before long we found ourselves peering out the airplane windows down at a small runway nestled between the imposing peaks of the Andes mountains.

The flight takes an hour from Cusco to Lima, and upon arrival the first thing you notice is the altitude. Cusco sits at 11,000 feet, and you constantly wonder why you're panting and out of breath after a short hike around the block at a moderate pace. The fact is, altitude can really mess with you, and you must consciously remember not to overexert yourself. Even a slow walking pace is enough to jack your heart rate up to near its maximum capacity. However, you don't *feel* as if you are going too hard, which is why you can get yourself into trouble.

Grady and I walked through the baggage-claim area of the airport and immediately were assaulted by the hordes of salesmen you find in all tourist areas in Latin America.

"Tours? Are you interested in tours?"

"Hotels?"

"I've got a special deal only for you!"

Although it sounds rude, the best thing to do is to stone-face anyone who offers you unwanted goods or service. If you respond with a polite "no thanks," they take the fact that you spoke as an opportunity to follow you and harass you until you buy something. Grady had a tendency to start reaching into his bag to hand out T-shirts and other knickknacks, but I dissuaded him with the assurance that the truly poverty-stricken areas were yet to come.

We pushed through the crowd and into the airport parking lot, where another horde of taxi drivers waited. Taxies conveniently waiting in the parking lot would be too expensive, so we hiked the extra two hundred yards to the street and flagged down a taxi there.

People say you should trust the taxies in the airport more than the random taxies on the street, but I've heard as many stories of people getting ripped off by airport taxies as by street taxies, so I never pay any attention to that advice. You can almost always get street taxies for half the price of the airport taxies.

"Plaza de Armas," I said, when we finally found a driver.

When traveling to an unknown city in South America, just ask for the Plaza de Armas. That's where everything is happening.

"Four soles," the driver responded.

We hopped in.

Cusco is one of those mountain cities where the sky is a striking blue and the sun is penetrating. Between the airport and the Plaza de Armas rests urban sprawl. You see many half-constructed buildings with rebar sticking up from the columns on the top floor. I was told that the reason so many buildings seem half finished is because under Peruvian law you needn't pay taxes until the building is complete. Naturally, a certain percentage of the populace never completes a building and in so doing, avoids paying taxes.

During the ten-minute taxi ride to the Plaza de Armas, the difference between the city center and the rest of Cusco is striking. The Plaza itself is a large square with a fountain and sitting areas. Around the Plaza, you find a plethora of ancient, beautiful Spanish churches built between elaborate walls of Inca construction. Many of the streets are barely wide enough to accommodate a horse and cart, yet cars race up and down them, honking their horns in impudent fury and scratching their paint on the tight corners. The fact that the roads are also winding and steep makes the city seem more like an elaborate labyrinth than a functional urban area.

We jumped out of our taxi and made our way to a cafe for a cup of coca-leaf tea. The tea is made from the same leaf that is used to make cocaine, and it's known to help with the altitude sickness. It's also recommended that you chew on the coca leaves themselves, which numb your lips slightly. Honestly, coca-leaf tea is a bit of a novelty. I think your altitude sickness is more affected by the sugar you pour into the cup than by the tea itself.

"Well," I said, "here we are."

Grady nodded and looked around in contentment.

"Is being here more relaxing than the typical military life?"

He smiled, and I could tell Perú was working its magic on him. He was outwardly calm, but I could detect the gears were turning beneath the surface.

An old man walked by, dressed in gray clothing. On his back he carried a bundle of sticks. He wore sandals that slipped on the slick concrete, but he always caught himself with surprising agility and continued on his way.

"Wouldn't it be nice," Grady said, "to give everything up and live a simple life like that?"

"I don't know," I replied. "That bundle of sticks looks pretty heavy."

"Some burdens are heavier," Grady said, sipping his tea.

Something seemed to weigh on him, but I didn't press for details.

People kept approaching to offer to take us on some kind of tour, but a tour was the last thing I wanted. I hadn't made the effort to live in Lima and learn Spanish so I could fork over a bunch of money to some tour guide. My goal wasn't to view Inca ruins while sitting in air-conditioned seats, gazing through the tinted windows of a brightly-painted bus. I wanted to hike through the ruins on my own and wander through whatever chambers or areas happened to entice me. I didn't want to hear some apathetic tour guide spurt, "No . . . don't go there," because he or she had seen the sight a million times and happened to be bored with it.

The only way to get a true experience is to be your own guide.

"Time to find a hotel," I said when we finished our tea. We scooped up our backpacks and headed to the first hotel we saw.

"How much per night?"

"Six hundred dollars."

I wasn't in the mood to be outclassed by a hotel clerk.

"Ha!" I snapped, putting on an air of indignation. "Excuse me, but I took this for an exclusive establishment. I wouldn't ever stay under the same roof with riffraff that could only afford to pay six hundred dollars a night!" With that, I turned on my heel and walked away.

"Really?" Grady said. "Six hundred dollars?" Grady was just as keen as I was to save money.

"Every room looks the same when your eyes are closed."

We started on a path that formed a concentric circle heading outward from the Plaza. We started looking for hotels that seemed a bit dingier.

"How much for a room?"

"Three hundred a night."

"One hundred a night."

"Fifty a night."

"Thirty a night."

Our spirits lifted as the doors continued to slam closed behind us. The numbers were getting better.

"Fifteen dollars a night."

"Ten dollars a night."

At that point we became curious as to how low it would go.

"Five dollars a night."

From there, they began quoting prices in soles. At one of these, we actually checked a room. It was a cozy little habitat in a building made of dried brick with no bathroom or heater, but a solid stack of blankets on the bed. As an experiment I locked the door and pulled it closed, then applied a light force to the wood just above the handle.

The door swung open.

I turned to Grady. "I think we should go back to the ten-dollars-a-night range."

He shrugged in agreement.

Still, it was good to know that in Cusco, you could spend as much or as little as you wanted. I came to learn that this realization applied to all things.

Chapter 22

Machu Picchu

The next day Grady and I headed out for the train to Aguas Calientes, the small city at the foot of Machu Picchu. The train station was next to an awesome market in Cusco that everybody tells you not to go to. The place is filled with plucked and gutted chickens hanging from the ceiling, alpaca clothing, and stands where they blended jungle frogs into shakes for your drinking pleasure.

We'd gotten our tickets the previous day at the *Estacion Huancho*, which was also a terrible hassle. Buying tickets always involves waiting around while some perpetually irritated person bashes away on a noisy keyboard while staring at an antiquated black screen with a green digital display.

"Can we get tickets for today?"

"Sold out."

"How about the day after tomorrow?"

"Only one available."

"How about tomorrow?"

"OK."

When you start worrying about the return trip, it really gets ugly. A universal business constant must be to reprimand helpful ticket salesmen throughout the world and fire them outright if their attitude continues.

The ticket agent asked to see our passports, but when they printed out the tickets, we noticed the numbers were all wrong.

"Excuse me, but this one has my name and his passport number, and his has . . ."

"Don't worry about it."

"But what if . . ."

"NEXT!"

If you try to protest further, the security guards are called.

Fortunately, we had no problems at the train station and were allowed to board without incident.

It's a three-and-a-half-hour train ride from Cusco to Aguas Calientes. The train itself is a quaint vehicle with comfortable, cushioned seats and large windows. The trip allows you to gaze out at the tremendous vistas of the Sacred Valley.

We were delighting in the trip, but about two hours in I started to get a little nervous. The countryside began to change from populated farmland to steaming untamed jungle. I'd just assumed there were going to be hotels out here, but I hadn't actually asked anyone — an oversight I now regretted.

As civilization continued to peel away outside the windows of our gently swaying car, I started forming tentative contingency plans. If necessary, I could crawl off until I found a place to burrow into fallen leaves and curl up into a ball. My other, poorer, ideas need not be repeated.

"I don't think we're going to find a hotel," Grady muttered glumly.

"Stay positive," I said, trying not to sound as if I'd been thinking the same thing for the last hour.

We fell into an uncomfortable silence, listening to the sounds of happy hikers all around us, muttering to each other in a dozen different languages. The topic of their conversation most likely was the marvelous peace of mind they enjoyed, their hotel reservations confirmed, and how stupid you'd have to be not to have a place to sleep lined up.

"Screw it!" I said, finally deciding to try false bravado. "We'll just go up there, see Machu Picchu, and die. I don't even want to think about what will happen after Machu Picchu. Hotels and reservations are only for punk tourists. We're here for the adventure! After Machu Picchu, we'll jump off the mountain and imbed ourselves in the earth!"

Grady wasn't as enthusiastic about these last remarks as he could have been, and we fell quiet again.

Our train came around the bend and halted. Here was a big green billboard welcoming us to Machu Picchu, but no other sign of civilization. The happy multitudes surrounding us began to stir and cluck like contented chickens. I hated them.

"There aren't any hotels," Grady said.

"Sure there are."

"Look out the window: only jungle."

"Do you think there are any poisonous spiders in there? I mean, spiders that people sleeping in the jungle would have to worry about?"

Before Grady could respond, the train chugged on around the bend. Suddenly, magically, before us stretched a small town of happy people waiting with open arms. The first sign on the first building that we could see said: *Hotel*. Grady was sufficiently pacified to give me the benefit of the doubt for at least a few more minutes. Once again, I had been spared.

The train stopped, and we jumped off. I hurried Grady along, keenly aware that this was the second train of the day, and if ever hotel rooms would be in short supply, that time was now. At the end of the platform waited a man in a smart uniform with a green sign reading: *La Pequena Casita*. He was in a group of about five other guys, all with similar signs.

"Do you have vacant rooms?"

"Yeah, sure."

A great surge of relief. "How much are they a night?"

"Twenty-five dollars." A second great surge of relief.

"Let's go."

The uniformed man led us down the narrow streets of Aguas Calientes, and guided us to our room. As I walked, I couldn't help but laugh at the punk tourists standing around, confused. Most were looking at their maps, trying to figure out how to find the hotel where they'd made reservations.

Free from the worry of where I would sleep that night, I took my first real look around the place and gasped.

Aguas Calientes is awesome. Green mountains rise straight up on all sides into a misty sky. A viscous river thunders along the border of the town, dropping easily a hundred feet within the course of a quarter mile. Along the roads wait street vendors in well-ordered huts, selling garments and blankets in the most vibrant colors imaginable.

The place reminded me of Adventureland in Disney World — that segment of the park where you can go on a "jungle safari", and where Swiss Family Robinson's tree-house is — but it reminded me of how I looked at Adventureland when I was ten years old, before I knew that Disney World was fake and plastic.

"This is the low tourist season, right?" I asked our guide.

"Yes," he responded, smiling and showing off several teeth surrounded by gold framework.

"Do tourists ever need hotel reservations, or can you always find a room here?"

Our uniformed guide smirked and shook his head 'no.'

"What happens when all the rooms are taken?" I pursued, because I had learned it was common in South America for people to respond without really listening.

"Only in the high tourist season could that happen, in June or July, but not now," he replied.

I was satisfied. We came to our hotel. Our room was lovely, with a view of the river. Grady laughed at how nice it was, noting that we couldn't get an equal room in the US for less than $150 per night.

"Fortune favors the ill-prepared," I laughed. "Now let's go and see that stupid Machu Picchu thing everybody keeps nagging me about."

Throughout the time I'd lived in Perú, everybody I knew (both Peruvians and those from the United States) kept scolding me that I hadn't yet been to Machu Picchu. I had been chastised so much for not seeing the place that this failure on my part had become a point of pride: I was not a gringo tourist. I'd come to Perú to learn Spanish and experience a different culture. Doing touristy stuff didn't appeal to me. The arrogance of the assumption that the only "good" things can be seen in a couple of days is a belief I find detestable.

What about the ambiance of a place? Sometimes you need a full year just to become aware of the general vibe, then another year or so to let the sensation soak in. People are drawn to places because of the famous sites, but the real treasures are always to be found in the local population.

Grady and I took our small backpacks and headed down the street to the buses. Machu Picchu is a 20-minute uphill ride from Aguas Calientes. A seat on the bus costs $9 round trip, a distressingly high price considering what you can get in Perú for $9. Prices quoted in dollars tended to be high for the value of the services rendered. Realizing that, we decided to forgo the bus and just hike up to the top.

We set off down the road with various people yelling and waving at us that we were making the worst mistake of our lives.

The only traffic on the road consisted of tour buses hurtling along with absolutely no regard for pedestrians who refused to pay the $9 bus fee. Grady and I took turns throwing ourselves into ditches or plastering our bodies against the sheer rock faces lining the road. Eventually, we stumbled across a rocky path with a rusted arrow that pointed up.

"Machu Picchu" it read, in barely legible letters.

Perfect, I thought. *What could possibly go wrong?*

The stairs went up and up through the seething, respiring jungle. About an hour later, we found ourselves at the entryway to the famous Inca city. The real ruins were still hidden behind the annoying turnstiles of authority that pop up around everything worth seeing anywhere in the world. No matter what people or natural forces conspire to make something miraculous, the same group of bureaucrats come muscling in to ensure no travelers can enjoy it until after a fee has been extracted.

Today you can no longer purchase a ticket at the entry gate, but back then the bureaucrats were less powerful, and the locals arranged things to be more or less convenient. We paid, walked in, rounded the first bend, and there it was! Just like in all the pictures you've seen. Instantly, I kicked myself as a fool for not having made the trip sooner. The Lost City was so grand and perfect that it didn't seem real.

The ruins alone don't make Machu Picchu amazing; the combination of mountains, layout, and wind coming up from below do that. Everything conspires to create a magical ambiance unlike anywhere else. The sight reminded me of Elven villages from *The Lord of the Rings*.

Here was a setting of enormous aesthetic power. Beauty for beauty's sake. Committed people in antiquity had built a city on the top of that mountain. The city might have added nothing to the bottom line, nor increased profit or production, but it does own an absolute beauty. The human spirit soars to be there. As you come upon the remains of that ancient settlement, you meet a spirit, a resolve essentially human, expressed in those rocks and that location.

Grady and I began crawling over the boulders and ancient stonework like little kids. We climbed up and down the terraces and took pictures of each other getting dangerously close to sheer cliff faces and edges that dropped off abruptly into nothingness. Machu Picchu is dissimilar to parks in the United States, where your sightseeing walk is dictated and every potential danger marked off with ropes and patrolled by watchful guards. Machu Picchu remains open, free, and the air rushes through the silent gray walls carrying a sensation of joy. As you walk and climb the green terraces, you smell the spirit of liberty much stronger than in other places, where the adventurous spirit has been lost largely due to fears of legal liability.

Intermittently the mountain rains came, but never lasted long, and the changing light gave us new photo opportunities. We climbed up the altar, sat under the tree in the courtyard, upset a mama llama and her baby, examined the sacred stone, and hoped to scale the mountain at the city's back, but we were too late: the guarded gate was closed and locked.

By then I wanted to stay at Machu Picchu for a month or a year or longer. I wanted to put up a little tent there and start terrace farming again. I wanted to run down the mountain and fish in the raging river, or bathe in the series of elegant stone baths in the ruins where water yet runs through the center of the complex. The stonework is so expertly constructed that the drainage system remains quietly functional, although the city has been abandoned for hundreds of years.

We finished our tour and returned to Aguas Calientes by hiking down the same stairs we had climbed that morning.

The tour book said you only needed one day to see Machu Picchu; that you could go to Aguas Calientes in the morning, tour the ruins, and then return to Cusco on the 3:30 evening train. Having now seen the ruins, that schedule seemed absurd. Walking along back toward the village, I found myself wishing I'd planned to stay for several additional nights.

Two days aren't enough time to see Machu Picchu, or two weeks. As we made our way back to the hotel, I wished we hadn't found a room and decided instead to curl up secretly inside the ruins. I wonder what kind of dreams we might have had, sleeping up there in that ancient place where people lived so long ago. I wondered how the wind, rising up along the green mountains, would stimulate your spirit when you surrendered yourself to slumber. That call of spirit had prompted me to embark on my travels with no clear plan. Maybe life turns out better if you just leave everything to chance.

I didn't know. I only knew that the bed was warm at *La Pequena Casita*, and that the Lost City was watching over me from the mountain above. Grady and I had taken our pictures and seen the designated tourist spots, but there was more to Machu Picchu that I intended to explore. For me, there are few places in the world that can change you in one night. Machu Picchu is definitely on that list. I resolved to go there again soon, if only to see what else might be revealed.

Chapter 23

Dancing in Barranco

By the time we got back to Lima, Grady was almost completely out of luggage. Every time we met a small child on a country road, Grady would pull a shirt or a hat or a pair of pants from his bag to give away. He still had one outfit left for his last night in Perú, so we began looking for something to do.

"It's Saturday," I said. "Let's go out dancing."

"I don't dance," Grady replied.

His was the typical gringo response, a result of living in the US where often times it felt like people only enticed you out on a dance floor to humiliate you.

"Dancing here is not like dancing back home," I assured him.

"How so?"

"Here, the mark of a good dancer is somebody who can make an inexperienced dancer look graceful."

Grady was still skeptical but he was an adventurous sort, so he agreed to give it a try.

We took a walk down Ricardo Palma toward the Ovalo de Miraflores. Grady had oriented himself pretty well in Perú, but I wanted to make sure he understood the layout of the neighborhood.

"To get back home," I said, "just find a taxi and tell them to go to the Ovalo de Miraflores. That's convenient because all the taxi drivers know how to get here. From here you can walk back up to our lodging." I pointed out all the landmarks nearby.

"OK," Grady said.

He didn't even ask why I explained how to get back. He implicitly understood that it was possible we'd get separated and each find our own way home.

"When I get back to Marisol's house, I just ring the bell?" Grady asked.

"Yup, somebody will let you in. Or go have coffee at Cafe Haiti if it's getting early, and I'll find you there."

Game plan in place, we headed out.

In Perú, night life doesn't really start until midnight but once things get rolling, festivities don't stop until the sun comes up. It didn't take us long to find a good party. As always, the girls were beautiful. They wore fresher, sexier clothing than the elegant formal wear we'd seen at the wedding; but, as with the wedding, they'd managed to elevate their appearance to an art form.

Right away, a girl approached Grady.

"You look like Alejandro Sanz," she said with a smile.

"Who's that?" Grady replied.

The girl laughed.

Soon she'd pulled him onto the dance floor where the two of them were swept along by the rhythms of the music to drift gently among the flowing crowd.

She was a good dancer: she made him look graceful.

As the night went on, and as expected, I completely lost track of Grady. I drank. I danced until the lights came on, and I was told to go home.

Taking a taxi to the Ovalo de Miraflores, I watched the sleeping city pass by through the smeared window. I felt the occasional flicker of concern for Grady, but I was fairly confident he'd be OK. He was a military man; he'd been trained to handle more difficult things than a simple night on the town.

I walked down Ricardo Palma, arrived at my house, and was just about to put the key in the door when I decided to have one more look around before I went inside. Turning on my heel, I headed down the road. In just a few minutes, a shadowy figure appeared in the distance.

Squinting, I couldn't help but wonder if I was about to be robbed. But as the figure approached, he became more recognizable.

"Grady!" I said, and suddenly burst out laughing.

Grady started laughing as well.

"Holy smokes," I said, "that worked out perfectly!"

"Yeah, I was just coming to see if I could find you and, if not, head back to get a hotel."

"How did your night turn out?"

"Incredible," he said, "absolutely incredible."

*

The next day, when I dropped Grady off at the airport, he seemed a little lighter than he'd been when I picked him up, spiritually speaking.

"You've lost weight," I remarked.

Grady grinned. "I'll come back. I should have some free time in a couple months."

"I hope you do."

We embraced, and he headed out to catch his flight.

As I watched him go, I couldn't help but feel a little envious. Grady had it all figured out. He had a good job and a great pension waiting for him when he reached retirement age. His future was secure, and anyone would be happy to call him brother or friend. According to the social code that had been instilled in us, Grady was doing it "right."

He had carefully and responsibly put everything in place to secure a stable life.

That life would have worked out great for him, too, if he hadn't been deployed to Afghanistan. There, all his generosity, intelligence and goodness was lost when he became a casualty of combat.

Chapter 24

Extending a Visa

My alarm went off, and I rolled over with a groan. Today would not be a good day. I knew this because I had to visit the immigrations office in Breña to extend my tourist visa.

Perú is a mellow country when it comes to border control. I'd heard stories of people staying in the country for decades under the designation of tourist. This is not technically breaking any laws, but a 30-year tourist status is not one you want to flaunt to government officials. Extending a visa meant drawing attention, and that had the potential to become problematic. No matter how kind and generous are the citizens of a nation, the bureaucrats always seem to be of a different breed. One should never rush to judgment on a nation based on interactions with agents of the local government.

The visa extension procedure has since been changed, but at the time the policy was as follows: Upon arriving in Perú you were issued a 90-day tourist visa. You could stay a total of 180 days on a single entry, provided you went down to the immigrations office in Breña to get three 30-day extensions. Each one of these extensions was called a *Prorroga de Residencia,* and could be obtained for about 30 dollars. The parameters were easy, navigating the system was the hard part.

Crawling out of bed, I hustled into some clothing and out into the gloomy, frigid morning. *Combis* flew down the road with a greater-than-normal indifference to the lives of passing pedestrians. I flagged one down and shuffled on board.

The immigrations office sits near the center of Lima, just down from Alphonso Ugarte. I stood in my *combi*, clutching a handrail, trying to maintain my balance as bodies bumped into me from all directions. After about an hour, I squeezed over to the door and out onto the street.

I had only walked a block down Calle España when I almost tripped over a mangy dog. The beast was lying in a pool of its own urine; it stared up at me with bloodshot eyes.

"Pleeeeeease kill me," it seemed to say.

I stepped over the unfortunate animal and continued along.

Well, this trip is off to a great start, I thought. My reflections were interrupted by the snapping teeth of that mangy dog, which suddenly came alive to attack me from behind. I broke into a sprint.

The dog's various maladies prevented it from catching me, and I counted myself lucky.

First obstacle of the day, hurdled.

Within a few minutes, I reached the immigrations office. The building hadn't opened yet. A throng of charlatans waited on the curb, attempting to sell forms available free of charge inside.

I dodged into a small copy shop to avoid them.

"Can I help you?" the attendant asked.

I produced my passport.

"Please give me two copies of my photo page, the entry stamp page, and my *tarjeta Andina.*"

The copy guy took my documents and set to work.

I always obtained a bunch of copies before entering the immigrations building. Better to have a multitude of copies of everything you could think of, otherwise the bureaucrats inside would keep sending you out to the street for more copies, in a concerted effort to waste precious time. The bureaucrats never thought ahead and told you to get all the copies at once because that would have been kind of them.

Copies in hand, I pushed through the throng of faux form sellers.

"F-007 form, sir?"

"No."

"But you need this!"

"No, I don't!"

At the door stood a metal detector and a guard.

"Purpose?" the guard barked.

"I'm here to extend my visa."

The guard motioned with his hand toward all four directions. Fortunately I had been here before, and knew that I must go to the desk immediately left of the security area.

Arriving at that desk involved waiting in line. You always have to wait in line, even if no one is lined up ahead of you. In that case, you wait behind a yellow line until the clerk at the desk deigns to recognize your existence. Sometimes the clerks willfully ignore you for long stretches. I suspect that they do this to make you drowsy. When they catch you nodding off they summon you forward in frantic irritation, as if *you* are wasting *their* time.

My patience remained intact, since I'd just entered the building, so I reached the first desk without incident.

The guy didn't ask me even one question; he stared at me as if I should know everything already. I fleetingly wondered how he'd worked himself into that mental state. You'd think if you worked at an information desk, you wouldn't be annoyed by people walking up to you and asking you questions.

"I'm here to extend my visa," I said.

The guy grabbed an F-007 form and lazily circled three sections for me to fill out.

"Third floor, window four," he said. Then he turned away. I was dead to him.

I had what I needed, so I made my way over to an uncomfortable desk provided for my inconvenience. I began filling in the circled sections on the form. The form itself included a maze of random boxes warning "DO NOT MAKE ANY MARKINGS HERE!" These boxes were haphazardly strewn across the whole document, and the information clerk had clipped most of these boxes with his haphazard circles in permanent ink. All that was required of me was to fill in my name and passport number and my address in Perú. I provided a fake address. What did they want that for? So they could come and abduct me in the middle of the night?

Completed form in hand, I climbed the stairs to reach the third floor.

Despite the fact that the building had only opened five minutes before, people waited in lines before numbered windows festooned with dust and cobwebs. Window four was no exception. I shuffled over and joined that line.

As I waited, I thought I'd play a video game on my cell phone. I pulled my phone out of my pocket, and flipped it open.

As soon as I did that, two armed guards tackled me.

"I'm sorry, sir," they declared in unison, "you may not use your cell phone here!"

They then snapped my cell phone closed, handed it back to me, saluted, and disappeared in between the lines of folk.

A few minutes later, somebody tried reading a book, with the same result. Apparently, any productive use of time was against the rules here.

Finally, a woman called me to the window.

"Purpose?"

A funny thing to ask: her window only served one function.

"I'm here to extend my visa."

"Oh, well, you need to go back down to the first floor and fill out form F-007." After saying this, she perkily looked toward the next person in line and started gesturing them forward. The only time a clerk at the immigrations office is in a hurry to see somebody is after they've just given you faulty information about what forms you need.

"I have that form," I said, and slapped it down on the table.

Her lips thinned into a disapproving straight line as she regarded the document. Her outrage over being forced to attend me now, instead of after a 30-minute break as I went to get a new form, was palpable.

She stood and looked over my form for about half an hour. I began to drift toward sleep again.

She noticed this and pounced: "You also need two copies of your passport photo page. Next!" she called in a rush, gesturing to the person behind me.

I had her, though. I whipped out the copies.

She scowled. She was really starting to hate me. Finally, after another 30-minute wait, she set about making the required entries on my form.

"Go down to the Banco de la Nacion and pay thirty dollars for the extension and fifteen soles to process the form. NEXT!" She glared past me, and her body language suggested any further questions on my part would be rude to those waiting in line behind me. Fortunately, I knew where the Banco de la Nacion was: back down the stairs, on the first floor.

I sighed, collected my papers, and descended the stairs. On my way, I checked my patience level, now hovering steadily at about 40%.

The Banco de la Nacion — national bank — has 30 windows for promptly attending people who must make payments. However, there are never more than two people sitting behind these windows taking money. Why any nation would want to inhibit people's willingness to fork over cash for idiotic services is beyond me, but I guess understanding that requires the evil genius of bureaucracy.

I found my place in line behind a species of mollusk thought to have been extinct for twelve centuries, and a human skeleton.

Waiting. Waiting. Waiting.

Occasionally, some attractive lady would come waltzing up and innocently go straight to the payment window, completely avoiding the line.

"Hey! Hey! Hey!" the waiting crowd called out. Then the security guard would step in and escort her to her proper place.

"Oh, I didn't realize there was a line . . . I'm so mortified."

Yeah, right: it's always an innocent mistake.

Finally, my turn came.

The clerks at both windows were unoccupied, sitting there scribbling away on papers.

I waited patiently.

After about ten minutes, one looked up. He seemed utterly flabbergasted to see someone waiting for him. That he had the nerve to suggest he'd had no idea that a line of people was waiting made me want to crush his voice box with my thumb and forefinger.

Instantly impatient, he began gesturing me to come forward.

"Come on, don't make all these people wait," he grumbled.

My left eye twitched. My patience level dropped another two percentage points. I stepped forward and handed him both forms and the pieces of paper that indicated what I was supposed to pay.

He told me the amount in soles.

At the national bank, you can only pay in soles, even though the fees are often quoted in dollars. If you don't have soles, you must leave, get some at another bank, then come back and wait in line again.

There's a reason I know this. This time I had soles. I paid.

The guy turned over a receipt and gestured furiously at me to leave quickly so he could begin ignoring the next person in line. This might be how the guy entertained himself; he probably spent his whole day laughing inside.

I tried to forget about him as I wearily trudged up the stairs again. I was getting close to the end of my mission, I reminded myself.

Back to visit my friend at window four.

After more waiting in line, she finally called me forward so she could scrutinize my various papers and receipts. "Passport!" she growled.

I handed her my passport.

She stamped it a couple times. This was encouraging, until she put the document in a huge pile of other passports. "OK, go sit down."

To be separated from your passport in a foreign country is unnerving, but she cared nothing about that.

I sat down and watched the second hand on the wall clock.

I had enough time to reflect on my whole life in real time. When I reached the current moment, I started making things up. Finally, they called my name.

I went forward.

"Here's your passport."

I took it.

"Get out of the way. Have you no courtesy for others who are waiting?" a demonic chorus of bureaucrats screamed.

The flashing red light of my low-patience alarm set off palpitations. They'd definitely gotten me to the point where I'd either suffer a heart attack or an implosion. But I had one last trick up my sleeve. "I'd just like to sincerely thank you all for your prompt and helpful attention," I said with a honey sweet smile.

The faces of 30 bureaucrats turned bright red in fury.

I chuckled and left the building, victorious.

Nothing is more offensive to a bureaucrat than good manners.

Chapter 25

Freelancing

On Calle Tarata squatted an internet cafe I frequented. The place was called the Dragon Cafe, and on the sign out front was a painted dragon curling into a circle around a stylized letter "D." Rows of computers sat on rickety desks separated by flimsy privacy panels. The chipping walls were painted white, and dust collected in the corners. At the cost of S/. 1 per hour, you could use the web. Every eleventh hour was free. The big advantage of the internet cafe was that it saved you from contracting for a monthly service.

I'd gotten out of the habit of getting into commitments that required monthly payments. Besides the rent and food, I had no expenses. It's liberating to come home and know there won't be a stack of bills waiting for you. This freedom came with certain inconveniences, but overall the trade worked for me. I liked that I needed to go for a twenty minute walk if I wanted to use the internet; it meant I wouldn't go online unless I had a true task pending that needed to

173

be taken care of. Not having easy access to the internet also prompted me to get lost in a book with greater frequency. Your brain feels better after staring at a book for a few hours than it does when you stare at a computer screen.

The computers at the Dragon Cafe were slow and outdated. Sometimes you'd type in the URL of the page you wanted, and stare at a turning hourglass for five minutes before the online page finally loaded.

On the keyboards, black with grime, the space bar always broke first. Typing anything using a faulty space bar creates a whole new dimension of irritation. A minor annoyance for people who can't type, but for fast typists a broken space bar is a highway of never-ending speed bumps.

The trick to navigating the Dragon Cafe was identifying the one or two fast machines in the cafe. If they were occupied, better to go somewhere else for an hour or so in hopes that they'd be available when you returned.

I also learned how to fix faulty keyboards. A metal wire spring under the space bar often became dislodged. Reattaching it took a few minutes but proved well worth the effort, even though the repair used up your own prepaid minutes.

I was submitting a lot of stories and articles for publication. I'd write on my laptop at home and save the files on a 3.5-inch floppy disk. When I got to the internet cafe, I'd attach the file to an outgoing email with "submission" in the subject header.

Internet cafes are breeding grounds for computer viruses. Neither the hardware nor software of internet computers is frequently disinfected. Inserting your 3.5-inch floppy disk into a cafe drive, and then later inserting this disk into your personal computer risked transferring all manner of malware.

The safest thing to do was load a file onto my drive, download it at the internet cafe, and then throw the disk away.

But I rarely did this: Disks were expensive.

On one occasion, I returned home to my laptop and inserted a disk, only to have my computer freeze up on me. Its screen went black, and although the green light next to the power button was glowing, my computer showed no other signs of digital life.

I pushed the power button a few times.

Nothing.

I tried unplugging the machine, but that was also ineffective. The computer simply went to battery power. But I had one final card up my sleeve: I flipped the computer over and pulled out its battery.

The laptop groaned and promptly died.

I sat there holding the carcass of my portable electronic brain and felt a shiver of fear which was more than just my concern over lost photos and files. My computer was my companion! It was the chronicle of my life! Without it, I would be alone.

I counted to thirty and jammed the battery back into the plastic body.

Nothing happened.

I replugged the outlet and pressed the power button. Soon I heard the familiar beeps and gurgles that always accompanied a start-up.

I was hopeful, but something wasn't right. The beeps and gurgles didn't sound the same. I waited.

In a short time the video screen turned completely blue. That couldn't be good.

"Resume operations in safe mode?" the computer asked.

I could toggle between the choices "yes" and "no."

I shrugged. I didn't know what safe mode was, but I craved the security being promised.

I toggled "yes."

The blue screen disappeared, and my desktop sprang back to life. It looked a little distorted; all its file icons were magnified. Still, everything was there. I could access my documents again.

Success!

Once I entered "safe mode," the computer become ever more resistant to the viruses I brought home daily.

I began placing articles, which was a nice supplement to my teaching income. Selling stories for between 20 and 100 dollars would barely pay for lunch in the US, but in Perú I could stretch out that cash for weeks. When a story was published, funds arrived in my PayPal account as instant cash. This became my regular routine, and each sale became a cause for celebration.

Chapter 26

Malaria Medications

After four years of living in Perú, I felt pretty comfortable. I spoke the language, knew a good group of locals who played basketball, and I continually met new people who'd join me for a drink in the evenings.

One night I was sitting in my room when I got a call from a German kid named Dirk. He was a tall, attractive guy with blond hair who sported a small piercing over his right eyebrow. Dirk was about 19, and he was spending a year traveling the world. Commonly, young people from all parts of the world spend a year or so traveling. It seemed that only in the US do certain classes regard young people who spend years abroad with suspicion.

Dirk wanted to see everything, do everything to make up for the fact that he was only 19 and short on life experience.

"Come on, man, where can we go? Tell me something you haven't done yet," Dirk insisted.

I thought for a moment. "Iquitos. I haven't been to Iquitos."

"What's Iquitos?"

"It's where the headwaters of the Amazon are. It's where Klaus Kinski filmed *Fitzcarraldo*."

"Aghhh!" To tease a German, you simply mention Klaus Kinski, the German actor who did all those films with Werner Herzog and spent as much time in mental asylums as out of them.

"I've heard there are a lot of pretty ladies in Iquitos."

This possibility convinced Dirk. A day later we both had tickets; we'd leave the next week. In the midst of my final preparations, I got an urgent phone call from Dirk:

"Hey, man, have you had your yellow-fever inoculation?"

"No, why?"

"My tour book says you need it to go to Iquitos."

"Dang."

Down we went to the immunization center in the center of Lima. It was a dingy orange building that seemed to have been painted to represent the disease it was there to combat. We went inside, paid our fee, waited in the requisite lines, and eventually saw the doctor. The shots were quick and painless. We were each handed a little yellow booklet verifying that we'd received the injections. These, we would have to show at the airport in order to get on the plane.

"This inoculation is not one hundred percent effective for ten days," the physician said.

"But we'll be in Iquitos in seven days," Dirk said.

"I guess you'll only be 70 percent protected."

"Great." I guess we were stuck taking the risk. Another problem solved.

The next day, my phone rang again. This time I was out hiking around the streets of Miraflores.

"Hey, I've just been reading my tour book again . . ."

"I hate it when you do that; it gets me all paranoid."

"Yeah . . . Um, it says here there's malaria in Iquitos. Can we get a shot for that?"

"I think so," I told Dirk.

"OK, why don't you see what you can find out, and I'll do the same, and we'll compare notes later."

"Right," I promised him.

The first place I went to do some research was the internet. I sat down at one of the fast machines at the Dragon internet cafe and typed "Malaria" into the search engine. I quickly learned that the internet is the worst place to go if you want some reasonable information about a disease. Every hysterical moron that ever lived has posted their most delusional horror story on the internet for innocent young travelers to find. A half hour later, I left the internet cafe white-faced, having read a dozen malaria horror stories about people dying or losing their hands to slow body rot.

My phone started to vibrate and flash green lights; it was Dirk calling again.

"Any progress?"

"Nothing good so far. I'm heading to the pharmacy now." The pharmacy was a good idea: pharmacists often know what prophylactic or curative drugs you should take. In Perú, where you don't necessarily need prescriptions, pharmacists are a valuable resource. I'd gotten into the habit of bypassing hospitals in favor of going straight to the pharmacy every time I felt sick.

"I'll meet you there."

I arrived at the pharmacy on the corner of Ricardo Palma and the Via Expressa. The pharmacy had floor to ceiling street-side windows that were tinted green. Dirk had not yet arrived, so I went straight to the girl behind the counter. Despite my confidence in Lima's pharmacies, success still depended on interacting with one of the more knowledgeable employees. It was about a fifty/fifty chance I would get one. The rest of the time . . .

"Do you have any anti-malaria pills or injections?" I asked.

The woman behind the counter stared at me blankly.

"Anti-malaria pills? Preventative medication? An injection?"

The woman finally came out of her stupor to reply. "No, no injection. We don't have anything like that."

A lesser man would have walked away, defeated. Luckily, I knew how to handle her.

"Why don't you check your computer?"

With a scowl of disgust, the woman pecked at her computer keyboard. Eventually she bustled off without a word to come back with a large bag containing small white pills.

These she handed me: "Take five a day for two weeks."

Just then, Dirk arrived. He was dressed in beige pants and a green shirt and had a canvas backpack slung over his right shoulder. "What's that?" he asked skeptically, looking at the bag I was holding.

"Those are my anti-malaria pills."

"Oh." Dirk fished in his backpack and pulled out a plastic card containing five pills.

"What's that?" I asked.

"These are what they gave me at the disease center. I'd take you there, but it's kind of a long trip from here. Actually, first they told me there was no such thing as anti-malaria medication. Then they gave me these."

"Well, there's only five."

"Yes, one a week for five weeks."

I eyeballed the big bag of pills the pharmacist had given me, each three times the size of one of Dirk's pills. I wondered, briefly, if my pills would have killed me had I taken them.

"No, I don't think I want those," I said to the pharmacist, and returned the bag to the counter. The pharmacist shrugged in annoyance and wandered off.

"Excuse me . . ." sounded a different voice.

I turned around and saw Dirk, the only other customer in the pharmacy.

"Are you looking for malaria medication?" came the strange voice again.

I finally realized that the pharmacy's security guard was speaking. He was standing in the corner in a kelly green uniform and tightly laced black military boots. He kind of faded into the green tint of the windows. "Why, yes. Is there an injection that you know of?" I preferred an injection to messing around with pills.

"Yes, of course there is."

I shot a look of triumph at the woman behind the register, but she was too busy staring off into space to notice. "Where?" I asked the guard.

"Go to the military hospital over in San Miguel."

"But we're not in the military."

"Doesn't matter."

I looked at Dirk, who shrugged. We thanked the guard and headed off into the street where we hailed a taxi. A little white sedan pulled up with a "taxi" sticker stuck in the window. After haggling over the price, we jumped in and started to make small talk as the vehicle weaved in and out of traffic.

"I've been reading about malaria," I told Dirk.

"Yeah?"

"It's nasty stuff. You can lose your hands."

"What was with those pills?" Dirk replied. "I mean, I get a packet of five pills, and you get a bag of fifty?"

We looked at each other and broke out laughing. When your life is at risk, you get no benefit from stressing.

Our journey required us to pass through several of Lima's districts, and it was fun to watch how the neighborhoods changed outside the window. We passed through San Isidro, a residential area that looked new, well-tended and very modern. It was clear there was a lot of money there. But then the taxi would cross a street and the region would become run down with prevalent graffiti on the walls and trash on the sidewalks; a few blocks later it would change again and we'd find ourselves on a busy street lined with commercial establishments like restaurants, gas stations, casinos and bars. In areas like these, there always seemed to be a wide selection of hotels and saunas with massive billboards advertising their location visible far off in the distance.

We'd just merged onto a multi-lane highway that passed through the center of a commercial area when we crested a rise to see a colonial-looking complex of buildings nestled into a little valley beside the road. The buildings were dark green with black trim around the windows. A black fence enclosed the area.

"What's that?" I asked the driver.

"That's the military hospital," he replied. He turned off the highway and pulled up next to a guard house. A man with a rifle leaned out a window and peered in at Dirk and me before waving us through. The exchange made me a little nervous. This seemed to be a pretty serious hospital.

The taxi driver dropped us off at a small roundabout in front of the main building and drove off in search of his next fare. We pushed open the large black doors and went inside. The place seemed strangely empty for such a large hospital. I couldn't escape the feeling we weren't supposed to be there.

Inside sat a gray-haired nurse behind a white desk. She was wearing dark-rimmed glasses and a frown. Aqua blue tiles extended halfway up the walls, and from there the walls were simply painted white. Behind the desk extended a poorly lit hallway where shadows abounded.

"Hello," I said to the woman. "We were told that we might be able to obtain some anti-malaria pills or injections here." I didn't add that I was given the information by a pharmacy security guard because suddenly that seemed totally ridiculous.

The nurse's reply was instant. "No," she said, so quickly that I knew she couldn't even have processed my question. There are days when you encounter nothing but helpful people, but those days are never memorable. It's not recommended to quit your quest after the first negative answer.

"I was informed that I could receive malaria medication here," I persisted.

"Well," the nurse replied, mollified, "let me check." It's a cultural norm in Perú that people sometimes tell you "no" before they have even processed what you're asking. There's no point in getting angry about it, and the behavior is not meant as a slight or an insult, it's simply the way they do things. Maybe they just say "no" to buy some time to think about your request since they know you're going to ask again. Maybe if you walked away after being told "no" only once they'd think you a lunatic. Once again I had to remind myself that my impression that the nurse was being dishonest or rude was an incorrect, ethnocentric judgment on my part.

Still, my own cultural response to things was not so easy to ignore, and I had to dispel my frustration. I took a deep breath and shook my head. Dirk, who was well-aware of all the cultural disconnect taking place, started to giggle.

"Go down there," the nurse said finally after consulting her computer. She made a vague motion of her hand to indicate direction. I didn't bother to ask for clarification.

We went down the hall, wandered around fruitlessly, and came back to the admissions desk. The gray-haired nurse looked vaguely annoyed that we had returned. She sighed in frustration because she might need to address my problem. Then she made a series of phone calls.

Eventually, another nurse appeared; this one was an attractive young woman who was spry and helpful. It had already been a long day, and meeting her was a relief. She listened intently as I explained the situation.

"Oh, follow me," she said with a smile.

We followed her down winding hall after winding hall of aqua blue hospital tiles. In section after section, heads behind small windows shook slowly in sad negation. We'd turned all the questioning over to our guide, and she was tireless. With every negative answer the nurse's resolve only seemed to strengthen as she continued on in pursuit of our goal.

I felt guilty for monopolizing so much of her time.

Suddenly, we turned down a dark alley at the back of the hospital. There we saw a sign reading "Malaria Center."

My eyes watered in childlike joy. Then annoyance set in. "Wait a minute: there's a malaria center in this hospital?"

Dirk, wise soul, laughed.

I didn't. "We went to fifty different wings, talked to a hundred secretaries, and not one of them knew of a malaria center in their own hospital? Not one of them could tell us, 'Go down that hallway, take a right'?"

Dirk nearly doubled over.

Our guiding nurse stood triumphantly beside the malaria center's door. I ceremoniously motioned her to take us inside.

She knocked on the door gently, followed by an experimental push.

Two women, one middle-aged and one young, looked up from a game of checkers in sleepy surprise.

"Yes?" the middle-aged one said.

"Hello," said our guide to the others in nurse's uniforms, "these young men want to know about malaria."

Initially, the two didn't react; then: "Come in, come in, come in; sit down, sit down," they said, bustling about like two sister tornadoes. They even made our guiding nurse come in and sit, as if she had nothing better to do.

The malaria experts set up a presentation board.

"Wait, wait," I told them. "We only want an anti-malaria injection or some preventative pills."

The women laughed sweetly, like I was the world's biggest fool.

"Oh, my dear, we have no anti-malaria pill or injection."

I felt my face heat with anger. Dirk let out a squawk of laughter.

"We *know* there is such a thing as —"

But the nurses interrupted: "We'll give you our presentation about malaria," they said sweetly.

I might as well have been Odysseus, trapped by Calypso. I was dealing with a force of nature beyond my power to deter. My only good choice was to limit my stress, sit back, and endure the lecture.

The women smiled now that they had established who was in control. They chattered for a moment among themselves and then began their presentation, which consisted of a series of cloth drapes painted with cartoons. The first cartoon depicted a giant mosquito with big eyes and a friendly smile.

I sighed in disgust.

Dirk stifled a giggle.

"Malaria is carried by mosquitoes in tropical regions of the world," one nurse began.

"We know how malaria is carried," I groaned.

"Shhh," the other nurse motioned sternly.

They flipped over the first drape to expose the second, showing a new cartoon of a sick-looking Peruvian guy.

"The symptoms of malaria are fever, stomach-ache . . ."

I made a "continue" motion with my hand. "Yes, we know what malaria is. We need to know how to not get it. Can you skip ahead?"

The nurse frowned, but she flipped to the next image. "To avoid malaria, do not get bitten by a mosquito."

Dirk slapped his knee. He was laughing so hard tears were coming to his eyes.

"Well, obviously, but that's kind of hard to —"

The nurse interrupted, raising her eyebrow.

"Mosquitoes breed in standing water, so drain all pools of standing water in your living area."

"We're going to Iquitos! We can't drain all the standing water in Iquitos!"

"You should wear long-sleeve shirts."

I nodded. That tip was useful.

The two nurses flipped over to the next page. In large letters on this drape were the words, "Always remember to take your preventative anti-malaria medication."

I sat up and pointed. "Yes, this one, tell us about this one."

The two nurses looked at each other and then flipped the page.

"Just ignore that last one, you weren't meant to see it."

"Aghhhhh!" I screamed.

An hour later, we left the military hospital. I'd had enough. I ended up at the nearest internet cafe, searching for the US Department of Health and Human Services website. There I found a list of 20 different anti-malaria medications. I wrote them down and stalked into the first pharmacy I could find, with the name of the first malaria medication on my list. This pharmacy was decorated with white and orange lettering on the signs and decor. "Lariam, do you have Lariam?" I asked.

"Yes," said a clerk in a smart white and orange uniform, handing over a white box. "Take one a day for five weeks."

"Great," I said. This wasn't the same medication Dirk had, but I bought it.

I took the pills. They made me feel like I was going to have a heart attack and gave me nightmares.

"To heck with it," I told Dirk. "I'd rather die from malaria than because of the preventative medication."

Dirk agreed. But his dosage was only one pill per week, so he kept taking his.

Chapter 27

Ayahuasca

Looking through the airplane window on the approach to Iquitos revealed terrain like nothing I'd ever seen. The jungle spread out flat in every direction with the uniformity only occasionally disrupted by an exceptionally tall tree. Through it all wound the brown water of various Amazon tributaries. The paths of these waterways seemed entirely haphazard, curling and twisting about in random patterns that folded back on themselves, coming ever so close to touching before turning away to spiral off randomly once again. The paths reminded me of veins in an organ.

We landed without incident and awaited our bags in the reclaim area before proceeding out to the concourse. The airport at Iquitos seemed to have been built on the same ground plan as the Jorge Chavez international airport, but at one tenth the scale. Standing at one end of the airport, a baseball could be sent to the other side with no more effort than a casual toss. It was comforting to arrive at a place with such a manageable airport.

The sliding glass doors opened at the exit and we were hit by a wall of humidity like walking into an invisible cloud. There were no cars in the parking lot, but rather mototaxies, each decorated with customizable decals. We picked one sporting the Batman logo, and hopped in, directing our driver to take us to the center of Iquitos. In a few minutes, we were standing on a boardwalk examining an indomitable body of water: the Amazon river.

It was beautiful. The Amazon holds a primordial power beyond anything I have previously witnessed. The river was huge and untamable, a living thing. Not even the mighty Mississippi compares to its majesty.

My eyes happened to fall on the Klaus Kinski restaurant overlooking the river. "Let's eat there," I said.

"No!"

"Oh, come on!"

And in we went. On each table was a placemat with a picture of Kinski looking like his deranged old self.

Dirk looked at his placemat and shook his head. "Look at him, he's completely crazy."

"That's what I like about the guy."

The menu featured alligator, anaconda, tortoise, piranha, and all other manner of jungle goodies and insects. I ordered a fruit shake, which was delicious.

Out in the water, a host of pink freshwater dolphins frolicked in the waves. They were also on the menu. I hadn't known they existed until one of them jumped out of the water, whistling at us.

Despite years of watching various nature shows on television, I'd never heard of the freshwater dolphins of the Amazon.

After lunch, we chartered a jungle tour from an ex-commando named Jorge. Jorge loaded us into a speedboat and we set off across the vast Amazon stretching as far as the eye could see.

We bounced along in the wake of old barges that were filled with an eclectic mixture of tourists in fancy clothing and bronze-skinned locals wearing only threadbare jean shorts. They waved at us as we passed by. We waved back.

Jorge took us to a small lodge in the middle of the jungle. The lodge overlooked a tributary called Rio Negro, and true to its name, the water ran pitch black. Looking beyond the hull of the boat, I noticed a huge mushroom cloud in the water that marked the spot where Rio Negro's currents mixed with the Amazon.

The lodge, designated as "luxury" quarters in Jorge's brochure, stood on stilts to keep it above the high water mark. Jorge explained that the water level here could vary by as much as ten feet.

"Ten *feet?*" I asked, not believing my ears.

Jorge only nodded.

Such fluctuations had left a stain on the stilts of the hut, approximately ten feet above the current water line. I could only shake my head.

When we opened the door to the lodge, the accommodations seemed nice enough. Mosquito nets draped doors and windows. Up in the rafters lurked at least two huge and hairy black spiders about the size of my hand. I pointed at them.

"Those are harmless," Jorge reassured me. "The mosquitoes are a big problem. Make sure you shut the door tightly at night or they'll eat you alive."

The lodge boasted a flushable toilet. The flush toilet is what allowed the lodging to be designated as "luxury."

Jorge then introduced us to the caretaker of the place, a small river-dweller named Javier.

"Javier will attend to all your needs," Jorge said. "I'll be back in three days."

With that, Jorge jumped back into his boat and sped away.

Javier smiled at us. "Are you hungry?" he asked in a whisper.

*

We dined on an excellent concoction of fried bananas and fish. Afterward, Javier decided to take us even deeper into the jungle, on an excursion to visit the local shaman.

We climbed into a tiny boat, and Javier paddled through dark waters, keeping the boat close to the shore where he could avoid the current and make progress both up- and downstream with comparable ease.

Rowing to the shaman's dwelling took about an hour. All at once, the thickly overgrown shore peeled back to reveal a well-tended clearing. Structures on stilts punctuated the harbor inlet. Kids played soccer in a central field.

"This way," Javier said, tying up the boat.

We followed him along a muddy trail that wound through lush green underbrush. The sun, disappearing below the horizon, threw rays of red light that painted the jungle with fire.

At last we emerged into a solitary clearing containing only one small hut. This hut was also on stilts, but these stilts weren't as tall. Apparently the construction site had been selected for its relative elevation.

The hut had a waist-high wall, but no windows or mosquito nets. After what Jorge had said about mosquitoes, I wondered how the shaman survived. The roof of the hut gleamed with corrugated metal.

Javier called out — not a shout but an elevated whisper, so in tune with the natural noises of the surroundings that few would recognize Javier's call as foreign from the background jungle noise. Nevertheless, Javier's whisper was met by an answering call, equally subdued.

Now I felt embarrassed by my own booming voice, cultivated through years of speaking over combustion engines and the horns of traffic. Even a refrigerator's buzz would have been deafening in the silent jungle. I tried whispering, but even my best efforts were discordant, falling far short of the natural-sounding calls made by Javier and the whispering shaman who, so far, had not shown his face.

Finally, the shaman emerged from the shadows of his hut, standing on his top step, barefoot, wearing a stained yellow shirt with a collar. He smiled and his coarse black hair and beard framed his twinkling eyes.

"Hello," he murmured, before he motioned us inside, remarking that soon it would rain.

I noticed several dogs milling about the stairs to the hut; they scurried underneath its shelter as the first raindrops began to fall.

"Even dogs know enough to get out of the rain," I said.

"Dogs, too, are intelligent," the shaman agreed.

In the center of the shaman's hut crackled a fire in a metal brazier. The shaman shuffled us over to the flames, whispering as he moved, as if he took care not to affront the natural world by speaking loudly, as if things lurking in the shadows might take offense at too much noise. "Every plant and animal in the jungle has a spirit," he said on a breath. "They come to me and tell me how to cure people of their ailments."

"And how do you communicate with these spirits?" I asked.

"This plant," the shaman said proudly, holding up a green, leafy mass. "From this I can make *ayahuasca*." He nodded to himself in bemused satisfaction.

"What's *ayahuasca*?" Dirk asked.

That seemed to be the question the shaman was waiting for.

"*Ayahuasca* is the spirit guide. When you take *ayahuasca*, you leave your body; you can travel to the farthest regions of the world; you can go to Europe if you want to, or Asia, or Africa. You can go anywhere."

I shared a quick look with Dirk, the description seemed as ominous as it was enticing. "*Ayahuasca* is a hallucinogenic drug," I said in a whisper.

Darkness fell quickly on the river. In darkness, the jungle became noisy. Sitting there, in that moment, I realized that civilization could never conquer the rainforest. All attempts would be flushed away by ten feet of rising water, or more.

"There are many different types of *ayahuasca*. There's *lobo ayahuasca*, *aguila ayahuasca*, *tortuga ayahuasca* . . ." said the shaman, his voice trailing off into silence.

I recalled a story about Allan Ginsberg or William Burroughs coming down to Perú to try some jungle drugs. Perhaps this *ayahuasca* of which this crazy shaman spoke.

"What do you do, as a shaman?" Dirk asked, clearly intrigued by the man.

"When people are sick, they come to me with their problems. Then I take *ayahuasca*, and it shows me what is wrong. When I know what is wrong, I go into the jungle. Then I take more *ayahuasca*, so I can find the plants I'll use to cure them. When I have the plants, I take more *ayahuasca*, to help me mix the ingredients into the proper medicine."

"So, basically," I said to Dirk in a low voice, "you come to him sick, and he gets stoned three times, makes some potion out of weeds, and gives it to you. Then you pay him. Sounds like a pretty good gig."

Dirk was less dismissive. "How did you become a shaman?"

"I went into the jungle for four years," the shaman said, solemnly holding up his hand with four fingers flickering in the firelight. "And every day for those four years, I drank *ayahuasca*. Imagine!"

"I can," I said. "It sounds just like college."

That comment elicited a giggle from Dirk.

Then came the bombshell: "If you want to try *ayahuasca*," the shaman said, "I can be your spirit guide. This journey is too dangerous without a guide."

"No thanks," I said without hesitation, knowing full well that the jungle medicine could be extremely potent. Dirk, however, hesitated. "Don't tell me —" I started to say.

But Dirk cut me off. "What? This sounds interesting." His voice was pensive but passionate. I sighed, wondering how to handle this. It wasn't my place to tell Dirk what to do, but taking *ayahuasca* didn't seem like the smartest move. Finally, I found my voice:

"Dirk, I'm not going to tell you not to try the drug, but I will say this: I've had some experience with this sort of thing and, let me warn you, this could completely change your life — and there's no guarantee it will be for the better. Before you do something radical, ask yourself how you feel about the way things are going. If you're miserable, verging on suicide or whatever, then I'd say, 'Heck, yeah. Go for it. Shake it up.' But if you're generally happy, perhaps it's better to consider a prudent course in which you ride that wave as long as you can."

Dirk nodded and sighed deeply, his youthful enthusiasm ebbing.

"And another thing to remember," I continued, "is that we're a day's journey from any hospital and a two-day trip from a good one. Plus," and at this I dropped my voice to a whisper, "I don't really trust that guy to make anything I'm going to ingest. He probably mixes his potions in a rusty oil barrel which he claimed as a prize after he discovered it floating down the river."

Dirk nodded.

"And?" the shaman asked quizzically.

"Um, no thanks, I'm not into *ayahuasca* right now," I said.

The shaman turned to Dirk.

"Me neither," Dirk said.

The shaman nodded in disappointment. It looked like he'd be tripping alone . . . again.

Our conversation turned melancholy for a time, until the shaman lightened up and started telling stories about other foreigners who had come here to try *ayahuasca*.

"There was this one time when a group of twelve Russians came here to take *ayahuasca*," he said with a big grin. "I was their spiritual guide, because it's very dangerous to take *ayahuasca* without a guide," he told us for the second time.

"Anyway, everybody was having a great experience, but one of them lay down on the table. No matter what I did, he just lay there and lay there and lay there. Finally, I went up and tapped him on the back. He went, 'GHAAAAAAA!'"

At this, the shaman pantomimed a prone Russian, springing up and making a face like a dead rodent.

"He went, 'GHAAAAAA!' and sprinted out into the jungle!" The shaman started giggling, a throaty, crackling, insane giggle.

"Wait a minute," I said, "you mean he went into the jungle?"

The shaman nodded.

"This same jungle? The one with the huge mosquitoes and jaguars and anacondas and things in it?"

Another nod.

"And aren't those things most active at night?"

Affirmative.

"And you just let him go?"

Now the shaman started chortling, holding his belly.

I shook my head. Jorge's warning about the mosquitoes came back to mind. I wondered if mosquitoes really could drink enough blood to kill you. What a way to go.

The shaman decided to try one final time. "So, are you two *sure* you don't want to take some *ayahuasca*?" He held up his little brown jug once more.

"No!"

This time our joint negation was definitive.

Chapter 28

Changing Money in Venezuela

Time seemed to accelerate. Before I knew it, I'd been in Perú five years. The people I met shuffled in and out of my life with greater and greater speed. Dirk hung out in Perú for a year, but then returned to Germany as was his plan, leaving only an open invitation for me to come visit him someday. I continued teaching, saving money and free time for the next adventure.

I needed new people to hang out with. When a friend gave up traveling and went back to "real" life, it always felt like a transition period, or the end of a chapter.

Shortly after Dirk left, I found myself perusing the internet for S/. 1 per hour, trying to self-diagnose several minor afflictions, when I came across a flashing announcement.

"The United States no longer recommends travel to Venezuela for US citizens."

I fished in my jacket pocket for my passport. Flipping through the ever-more-dingy pages, I came to the one with my Peruvian entry stamp.

As I'd dimly remembered, my visa would expire in three days.

My last visit to immigrations in Breña had convinced me that it was better to renew a visa by traveling to other countries instead of seeking repeated extensions.

Leaving four unelapsed minutes of internet time on the flickering tube screen, I hurried straight to the nearest travel agency.

"A ticket to Caracas, please."

"What class?"

"Cheap."

*

When recklessly traveling to foreign nations I know nothing about, I'm never nervous until about 20 minutes before landing. I can check in calmly, board without a hiccup, and endure take-off with nary a shudder, existing in my own dream world where I'm untouchable in my perfect fantasy.

But the second the pilot's voice on the intercom announces he's starting his final descent, the reoccurring doubts as to the wisdom of this audacious impulse spring back to life. No matter how I try to distance myself from social conditioning and unfounded preconceptions, doubt lurks just below the surface.

Oh my God, I'm going to Venezuela!

Not until 20 minutes before landing did I realize I didn't know anything about Venezuela. The whole impetus of my trip was reactionary: I didn't like the media telling me where to go and not to go.

I set to work on a mental checklist of potentially useful facts about the country. I knew that Chavez was the guy in charge. I knew that it "was not recommended" that Americans go there.

I also knew Venezuela tolerated a black market for US dollars: you could get a better exchange rate in the street than from the banks. Dirk had told me this; I hadn't bothered to verify it anywhere; researching on the internet always left me confused and discouraged, often convinced I was about to die of any number of obscure diseases.

I had come to prefer learning by experience.

The plane landed amid a beautiful sunset. The seat belt sign went off. Nobody moved.

Were these passengers terrified of offending the agents of Venezuela's police state? Some dark part of my brain imagined nearly inaudible "clicks" of sleepless government spy cameras, recording every move of every traveler in hopes of recording any transgression that could justify horrible punishment.

The plane rolled along the runway to the airport apron.

Eventually passengers stood, but by now I was looking at them suspiciously. Any one of them could be an enemy or informant. I slipped my backpack from the overhead compartment and elbowed my way down the aisle, deflecting anyone from planting a roll of microfilm or bag of cocaine in one of my pockets.

My fellow travelers shuffled along, with me in the middle of the crowd. I had no escape now. They don't let you stay on the plane after it lands.

Could I get through customs, blend into anonymity as I did in the line? I must bluff my way past the immigration desk. My passport said "U.S.A." in shiny letters. No customs clerk could overlook my citizenship.

I was done for.

I began to plan what I'd do with my newfound fame after being featured on "Locked up Abroad."

In record time, I found myself standing in front of a customs agent.

I reached forward with my passport in hand.

"Naw, that's OK, sir, you just go ahead."

"Really?"

"Yeah, really. We don't focus on that formal stuff all that much here in Venezuela. Enjoy your stay in our beautiful country!"

"Huh . . ."

I put my passport in my pocket and walked along. Most airports maintain a secondary "security" line, but not Caracas. In Caracas, you pass through a sliding glass door, and you're free of any government hassle. I had only to find a ride to take me down to the coast and the heart of the city.

"Taxi?" In the dusk outside, on the sidewalk, a sunglasses-clad fellow waved cheerfully.

"Sure," I said.

He made a gesture. I followed him. He wore brown pants and an ugly yellow shirt with a pocket over the left breast. As we made our way through the crowd of buzzing humanity always thronging at airports, I leaned over to the driver: "I heard you might be able to change some American dollars."

"Sure, sure, sure."

"What's the rate?"

"It's four thousand five hundred Bolivars to one dollar."

That sounded good. I vaguely remembered that the official rate was 2,600, so the taxi driver's offer was much better.

We kept walking.

The driver guided me into a dark and dilapidated-looking stairwell, exactly the type of place where zombies or extraterrestrials might drop on you from above.

"Where are we going?"

"Cab."

"Ok."

Down, down, down we went, the noble poet Virgil and I, abandoning all hope as we passed through the portal. The stairwell resembled the world's worst set of giant decaying teeth. Mold and darkness clawed the walls in a futile attempt to escape. Finally the taxi driver opened a door, revealing a parking garage.

This parking garage was even darker than the stairwell. A few lights flickered overhead, high up where the bulbs had not been shattered, perhaps by random gunfire. My imagination ran wild: I expected to see undercover immortals leap out of shadows, battling each other to the death in pursuit of victory in an ancient tournament of which modern society remained ignorant.

The yellow-shirted taxi driver trotted off into absolute darkness, his mirrored sunglasses remaining firmly in place no matter how black the surroundings.

The taxi driver stopped suddenly. "Car," he said. He popped open the trunk of a dirty white car.

Its trunk light came on to reveal a crumpled sheet of thick plastic. The driver pushed this aside, to expose, much to my surprise, piles and piles of money.

"Uh . . ."

"You wanted to change some dollars, right?" he asked.

I looked furtively over each shoulder, wondering if I were about to be shot in the back of the head.

"Yeah, how about two hundred dollars' worth?"

"Ok, ninety thousand Bolivars," the taxi driver said.

"No," I replied, "four thousand five hundred times two hundred is nine hundred thousand." Even in my state of borderline panic, I wasn't about to fall for the oldest trick in the South American book of techniques to squeeze money out of tourists. You never rely on the guy changing your money to do the math correctly. Never.

"Oh, ha ha. Yeah, you're right."

"Of course I'm right."

He handed me the 900,000 Bolivars. Now I was truly in jeopardy. It didn't matter that the wad of scrip only had the buying value of 200 US dollars; people kill for 900,000 of anything.

"What now?" I sighed, wary that he might throw the plastic on the ground, slit my throat, and wrap me up for a quick trip to the garbage dump.

"Now you get in the car, and I take you wherever you want to go."

"OK."

We got in the car. I dug out a card from a hotel someone in Perú had recommended, the Hotel Alta Mira, adjoining the Sambil shopping center.

"But not the good Alta Mira," I said, doing as I'd been advised. "Take me to the cheaper one that's just around the corner."

"I know it well," the driver replied, and we were off.

Night-lit Venezuela spread out before me like a twinkling diamond on the edge of the coast. In the dark, I could see the ocean, reflecting the stars and the glittering cityscape. We descended toward Alta Mira through a night as cool as lemonade chilled with fresh ice.

As we drove, I decided to ask the question that had become a point of contention back home.

"What do you think of Chavez?"

My time living abroad had taught me to regard all media reporting with cynicism. Truth could always be distilled from printed text or broadcast words, but real, useful information could only be extracted after considering the positions of the authors and the publications involved. There is a lot of misinformation in the media; whether that's a developing trend or if it has always been the case is a matter of debate. I was especially skeptical of those who resented my impulse for personally checking the facts.

Acquiring a second language had also opened up a whole new world of information-gathering. I'd learned that Spanish language publications often reported an incident with a completely different interpretation than their English language counterparts. I could see how a bilingual readership would make it more challenging for any single entity to control a narrative. There is no greater display of patriotism than to ensure you are basing your actions on the most accurate information possible.

The taxi driver shrugged in response to my question.

"Half the country likes him, half the country hates him," he said.

That sounded like every politician since the beginning of time.

I glanced out the window. A billboard caught my eye: "Don't vote for Chavez, and we'll clean our own toilets," it read. I couldn't tell if the ad was serious or sarcastic.

"So it's the poor that vote for Chavez?" I asked.

"He gives them free milk."

"How does he pay for it?"

"From the assets he seizes from rich people."

I didn't ask any more questions.

I ended up spending two wonderful months in Venezuela without suffering any kind of negative incident whatsoever. The fears I'd had about traveling there were unfounded.

Chapter 29

What Is Snow?

When I returned to Perú, I met a guy at the Corner Bar who told me they were hiring English teachers where he worked.

"It's called the Milton School. They pay pretty well."

By then I'd moved on from teaching at language institutes and I was offering private lessons instead, but the idea of working in a high school intrigued me. As a teacher, I'd concluded that rigidly enforcing authority created an ineffective learning environment: I'd had greater success engaging my students as equals and allowing them to dictate the flow of lessons. Professional teachers tended to disagree with me on this philosophy — but I had been getting good results.

Students are experts in how they, as individuals, learn; and the more I allowed the students to influence how I presented the material of the day, the more effectively it was absorbed.

But I had been working with adults more than children. So I was curious to test whether my methods would work with students at earlier stages of development. I was well aware that I risked utter disaster, but that had never stopped me before.

"Do you think I could design my own curriculum there?" I asked my new friend at the Corner.

"Absolutely. They're very accommodating to native English speakers."

I told him I was interested, and he made a call on my behalf. After a cursory interview, I got the job.

*

La Molina, one of Lima's 49 districts, is radically different from Miraflores. In Miraflores. a constant cloud sits right on top of the neighborhood, making it overcast, humid, and glum most of the time. In La Molina, however, the sun always shines.

The Milton School's massive complex had distinguished-looking ivy growing on its front gate — so much ivy that I had difficulty finding the door. I finally rapped on the wall.

A moment later a small slit opened, revealing a pair of curious eyes, followed by the door opening.

As in Los Olivos, the Milton School's rooms fronted on an open inner court, but the grounds here were better tended and greener. After a few days of administrative activities, I faced my first classroom filled with eager students beginning a new school year.

My students had attended total-immersion schools for their entire education. Still, I knew from experience that this didn't necessarily guarantee a sophisticated or highly developed comprehension of the language. I needed to choose a text which I could use to teach and evaluate my students simultaneously. The text had to be challenging enough to acknowledge their level, but easy enough that they could manage it.

I decided to start my most advanced classes with Jack London's *The Call of the Wild*. London's classic is written in straightforward language that non-native speakers could navigate with relative ease. The book also presents lofty themes for class discussion, important if the text proved too elementary for my students. However, my selection contained a stumbling block that I never anticipated.

One of the best methods I'd discovered for learning Spanish was to read along in a book while listening to a recorded narration, so you see the spelling of the words while listening to the pronunciation. The inflections of a good reader also express nuances of communication that you miss when studying printed text.

I handed out copies of the book and stood at the front of the class, reading the text as they followed along.

At first, the students found this activity novel. They'd listened to cassettes before, but they'd never had a teacher stand in front of them and read. Also, I encouraged them to stop me and ask questions. This gave them more freedom than they'd previously experienced in class.

Early on, a couple of the students got rowdy. I stopped my activities and threatened the entire class with my copy of Raymond Murphy's *English Grammar in Use*. Murphy's text is the go-to source for grammar exercises and a tremendous resource, but to say it's dry is like remarking that you're "a trifle parched" before keeling over from dehydration. "Look, class," I said, "you can either sit there quietly and listen to a story, or we can spend the day picking which of four grammatical options is most correct. It's up to you."

They instantly quieted down.

We plodded along through *The Call of the Wild*, students stopping me occasionally, asking for definitions or grammatical clarifications. I found their English to be very good. When they became immersed in the story, their questions became less frequent. They still heard words they didn't know, but by then they were absorbing the meaning through context. That's what I liked to see, since it meant they were taking ownership of their knowledge of the language — a difficult achievement in most educational settings.

The story progressed to the Yukon, where London's canine character, Buck, was getting his first taste of the cold, when a bright student named Gonzalo raised his hand. Gonzalo had already proven himself to be a joker.

"Yes, Gonzalo?" I said.

"Teacher, what is 'snow?'"

I waved my arms in exasperation. "Seriously, Gonzalo, the book is just getting good and you're interrupting with a question like that?"

I was surprised when Gonzalo flashed a hurt look at me.

"Wait a minute," I said, "you seriously don't know what snow is?"

Gonzalo shook his head.

"Who can help him?" I looked around the room.

By now, all the students had lifted their heads from the text, giving me blank looks.

"Seriously?" I thought about it for a while and produced the Spanish word for snow, which is "*nieve*."

The students shrugged.

For a native of Northern Wisconsin, the thought of whole populations being ignorant of snow was almost incomprehensible. Even after living in Perú for many snowflake free years, I hadn't explored the full ramifications of the concept. To endure the inevitability of Wisconsin winter, you develop a mental habit of not dwelling on the thought that the cold is coming. If the snow falls later than normal, you express gratitude for a few more days of life free from shoveling, but you never engage the idea that the winter will *never* arrive. Winter *always* comes.

But no snow ever fell in Lima.

It was so obvious I'd completely missed it. My mind was blown. I stumbled for a moment as I tried to figure out how to approach the problem.

"Have you ever seen a picture of a mountain?"

"Yes."

"Have you noticed the white stuff on top?"

"Yes."

"That's snow."

"Ahhhh," they said, and as one they all looked back at the book, ready to resume.

But I wasn't satisfied. What kind of a definition of snow was that? How could they not know about snow? It's said the Eskimos have over a hundred words for snow. Suddenly I was filled with an overwhelming nostalgia for my winter heritage. Snow is a spectacular and diverse phenomenon that forms the foundation of a plethora of activities essential to the human experience. Snow comes in many types: soft snow, wet snow, hard snow, fluffy snow, compact snow, corn snow. Snow is the stuff you have to shovel. Snow is for sledding, snowmobiling, building snowmen, and skiing! Snow covers cities like a blanket and makes roads impassible. Thinking about snow had taken up a good portion of my life since I was old enough to be swaddled in a snowsuit and sent outside in the pursuit of rosy cheeks.

But there was a more human element of concern provoked by this abysmal lack of knowledge. Something that chilled me to the bone.

What kind of kids don't know what it's like to wake up at six a.m. and see enormous flakes piling up on their windowsill? Flakes that make them run to the TV and scan through the channels until they find — joy of joys — that school has been canceled for the day?

A snow day! All due to wonderful, beautiful, pristine white mounds of glorious snow!

Really, they didn't know what that was like?

I suddenly felt an all-encompassing sense of pity for them.

"What about Christmas?" I asked.

"What about it?"

"What does Santa drive around in?"

"A sleigh."

"Ah-ha! Why a sleigh?"

Shrugs again.

"Because of the snow!"

Suddenly it occurred to me that perhaps they couldn't enjoy *The Call of the Wild* if they had no experience with snow.

I sat down, momentarily defeated.

"Teacher, what's the matter?"

I brushed the question away. "OK," I said, regaining my poise, "let's learn about snow. Do you know that water changes its form when the temperature changes?"

They looked at me as if I were a lunatic. Of course they knew *that*, everybody knew *that*. *That* was totally basic. How dare I even ask them *that*?

"What happens to water when it gets hot?"

"It turns to steam," somebody said.

"Right! Now, what happens when water freezes?"

Again the blank stares.

"You don't know what 'freeze' means?"

A bunch of heads shaking in the negative.

I fought down a surge of vertigo and looked for a teaching tactic. "OK, say it's a hot day, and you want some ice cubes for your Inca-Cola."

They were nodding; they were with me. Good.

"Where do you get ice cubes?"

"From the freezer," somebody said, but they said the Spanish word, which is "*congelador*." However, once the Spanish word was out there, I saw realization dawning in their eyes.

"Right! You put water in the freezer, where it's very, very cold. The freezer turns the water into ice." I finally felt as if I was gaining some momentum. "Now, there are places in the world where you don't need a freezer because it's cold enough to turn water into ice everywhere." I made an all-encompassing gesture. "You just put the ice-cube tray outside filled with water, and it becomes ice."

"No teacher, that's not possible."

"It is possible."

"Even water in the lakes?"

"Yes, the lakes too."

"What happens to the fish?"

"The whole lake doesn't freeze from top to bottom," I said. I was about to say more, but we were ranging far afield.

"This book," I said, holding up *The Call of the Wild*, "is set where it's so cold water turns to ice."

"You mean, it's set in the freezer?"

I was about to get frustrated again, but I paused. "Yeah, just pretend they're in the freezer, a giant freezer with mountains and frozen rivers and hundreds of miles of trails they have to travel."

"Wow," said a couple of the kids.

I started to smile. This class would be all right. One final moment of inspiration struck me. "I want you each to go home tonight and stick your hands in the freezer for a full minute. Then the next time Jack London mentions 'cold,' you'll know what he's talking about."

Chapter 30

Quieres Bailar?

Milton School provided a small teachers' lounge where the staff could grade papers, have lunch, or relax. It was a nice room with a large window that overlooked a little park. The window provided a soft, natural lighting that was easy on the eyes, which was a welcome break from the harsh, artificial light of the classrooms. Three other native English speakers worked at the school; nice guys, but different from those I met working at Los Olivos. These guys were more serious, more career focused, and less inclined to rush to the bar on payday and stay until closing.

Naturally, we native English speakers formed our own group and lunched together in the lounge.

One day, we were eating when a striking middle-school teacher entered and walked over to the table where the Spanish speaking teachers congregated. She was on her cell phone when she came into the lounge, giggling and deep in conversation. She flashed me a dazzling smile, and I later heard her admit that she liked to dress in a way that distracted drivers and caused accidents as she was walking down the street.

"Who's that?" one of my tablemates said.

"Azucena," somebody replied.

At the sound of her name, Azucena looked our way. We waved. She waved back.

"Wow, she's gorgeous," the original speaker continued. "Why didn't I see her at the in-service?"

"She just got hired," said another.

Azucena continued to throw us looks as she ate her lunch.

The teachers' lounge was suddenly far more interesting.

*

The assumption among the Peruvian teachers at Milton School was that the native English-language teachers could not speak Spanish. Throughout Perú, including the various language institutes, most native English teachers were backpackers whiling away a few months abroad.

The rule held true among our group at Milton School. One of our native speakers didn't know a single word in Spanish. The other two knew enough words to do such things as get taxies or order dinner but had no conversational fluency.

I was the exception.

At that point I'd been in Perú for over half a decade, and spent most of my time exclusively with Peruvians. I'd finally achieved a level of linguistic fluency that allowed me to enjoy local television. However, at Milton School we were encouraged to speak only in

English, so I hadn't made my Spanish fluency widely known.

This meant that when people were speaking about me, I could understand them.

One day, Azucena entered the teachers' lounge, smiling, and sat among her friends.

"*Vaya*," she said, "have you ever noticed how attractive that American teacher is?"

"Which one?"

"That one on the end in the blue shirt with the dark hair."

"Yes, he's gorgeous."

I took a quick bite of my sandwich, because I was the teacher with the dark hair and the blue shirt.

"Wait a minute," one of the girls said, "do you think he understands us?"

"Oh, come on," Azucena replied. "He's super American, and no Americans speak Spanish."

"I suppose you're right."

A round of giggling ensued.

I looked up innocently and smiled. "Is everything all right?" I said in English.

"Absolutely," they said back.

"Now, you know what I'd like to do," Azucena said, reverting to Spanish and lowering her voice a bit, but not so much that I couldn't hear. She then started in with a series of very appealing suggestions that made my cheeks flush.

"What's wrong with you?" one of the other English speakers said.

"Oh, nothing, nothing. This *aji* is a little hot, is all," I said, referring to my lunch. Nobody believed me for a second, but I wasn't going to give them details they'd have heard for themselves if they spoke Spanish. It served them right for not taking the time to learn the local language.

*

I kept my knowledge of Spanish hidden for a time, which takes discipline when you know an attractive woman is interested in you. I liked Fridays best, because on Fridays I stayed after classes to play soccer with the students. Azucena always stayed late, too. She said this was because she wanted to finish up her work for the weekend, but in Spanish she told her girlfriends she stayed because she liked the way I looked in shorts.

Two months into the school year, we had our first teacher-appreciation day, a party during which staff relaxed and had a few drinks. For the event, the Milton School's administration rented a large reunion hall and treated us teachers to dinner.

"Pssst," I said to the first waiter who served us.

"*Señor?*" he asked.

"Here," I replied, handing him a S/. 20 note. "Make sure we're the first to be served the next round of beer."

He smiled and palmed the cash. Everyone at our table started laughing.

A few minutes later, another waiter came up.

"Pssst," I said, and repeated my request.

Soon, waiters were stumbling over themselves to bring us beer.

"What's going on?" the teachers at the other tables yelled at our table, brimming with four full pitchers while they rationed quarter-full vessels of mostly suds.

I began to serve them from our pitchers to generate some goodwill. "Here, have some beer, my friend," I said, pouring.

As the night rolled on, waiters pushed away tables and the lights were dimmed: time to dance. If you're at a party in Perú, there will be dancing.

With a belly full of beer, I wandered over to Azucena's table. She'd been watching the waiters fawn over my little group but, unlike the rest, she seemed to think the situation amusing.

"Excuse me," I said, "would you like to dance?"

"Ye–" she started to say, but then stopped when she realized I'd spoken to her in Spanish.

"Wait a minute," she said. "Do you speak Spanish?"

"I'm more or less fluent," I continued, "although I do mix up my grammar occasionally, and get genders wrong."

By now, Azucena was red-faced.

"Go on. Dance with him," one of her friends said. "After all, he *knows* you want to."

I grinned.

Azucena took my hand.

She turned out to be the best dancer in all Perú.

Chapter 31

Creative Writing

My class became highly animated when we began the creative writing unit. By then, my students were producing three- to five-page compositions, which was something they'd never been required to do throughout their schooling. I explained how I would evaluate their short stories, then added a teaser at the end: "If any of you manage to sell your work," I said, "I will change your grade to a perfect score."

The students looked at me in disbelief.

"If you make a sale for as little as five dollars, you'll still have made a sale, and I'll change your grade. Now, this deal doesn't extend to those of you who have family in publishing, or wealthy uncles," I added as a caveat. "Your sale must be legitimate."

One of my students found his voice, a sharp kid named Alex who'd spent part of his life in the United States: "Would changing the grade be an admission that your first evaluation was wrong?"

I considered how to answer that. "Any evaluation is only an opinion," I said. "Many great novels were rejected for publication numerous times before they sold. The difference between a good school composition and one that you can market professionally is enormous. If you do the extra work of polishing your story and successfully selling a submission to a publisher, you'll have earned a perfect score in my book."

My students still seemed skeptical. I was changing the teacher-student relationship, and they didn't quite know how to react.

"I keep telling you to take ownership of your own education. Listen to criticism. Criticism represents an evaluation of you, yes, but you may evaluate that criticism in return. You can dismiss the critics whom you conclude do not provide you with insight or benefit. That includes your teachers. Educational relationships work better when both sides are empowered to participate."

A bright girl named Gaby raised her hand. "Isn't that attitude a little bit arrogant?" she asked.

I was impressed by how politely she worded a combative question. Gaby might have a career in politics ahead of her.

"It's only arrogant to dismiss all critique out of hand. To evaluate criticism on its own merits isn't arrogant, it's prudent."

You can tell when students still harbor doubts about what you're saying. Uneasiness fills the air. Worst of all, in such moments, the students become reluctant to question. I decided to present the idea another way. "Look," I said, "if I took off a point for every minor error you made in your compositions, you'd all end up with negative scores."

They stiffened at this, so I clarified: "Don't get me wrong, you're doing good work and showing improvement, but any teacher can find enough errors to justify a failing grade if that's all they are looking for."

"That's not fair," a student said.

"Exactly right! It's not fair, which is why you should guard yourself against unfair treatment. You must evaluate whether the teacher's evaluations are valuable."

"But shouldn't a student learn to avoid making mistakes?" Gaby asked.

"Yes," I said, impressed at her continued insight, "but not at the expense of your willingness to take risks."

Once again the students seemed to plummet into confusion.

"Look, you all know how to do basic sentence construction, right?"

They agreed that they did.

"Every time you write something, you choose between making a basic statement, which you know how to do well, or saying something more complicated, at the risk of making a grammatical error. If you have a teacher who pounces on every error, you won't attempt writing more advanced thoughts. Too great an emphasis on perfection limits you to expressing only basic ideas. I prefer that you challenge yourself by discussing complex concepts. I don't mind errors made as you push your comprehension of language and expand your own thinking. In fact, the presence of such errors may indicate an increased commitment to your own education."

The students sat quiet briefly, trying to wrap their minds around the idea of a teacher telling them not to be afraid of mistakes.

Alejandro, not the greatest student, piped up: "Don't be afraid of mistakes? How come I lose so many points on all my papers? How do you know I'm not just challenging myself?" Alejandro was an athletic kid with dusty blond hair who was popular with the girls. He spoke his question with a smirk.

"Because your errors are on basic stuff that you should know better."

"You mean you can tell the difference?"

"Yes."

"I think I'm going to dismiss your evaluation," Alejandro said. The students laughed.

I shrugged. "That's your right," I admitted. "Only time will tell if my advice to you is effective or not. I can't make you believe it; you'll decide if what I say has merit. I know this much though: most people who are trained to pursue a false sense of perfection become extremely risk-averse. Personally, I'd rather strive for error-riddled greatness than be limited to perfect mediocrity."

Chapter 32

Wayna Picchu

By the time the school year ended, I'd developed a sincere affection for all my students. I felt both sad to see the year end and happy because my teaching style yielded good results. It was a small statistical sampling, but I remained satisfied. The administrators at Milton School wanted me to come back for another year, but I decided to go back to private classes which entailed more freedom and less structure. Before scheduling any classes, I wanted time to think, so I bought a ticket for a solitary trip to Cusco where I'd scale Wayna Picchu.

Wayna Picchu is the mountain background of every picture ever taken of Machu Picchu. It's a strenuous climb, complete with rusted cables bolted into walls and ancient steps worn by time and countless visitors.

Every year the Wayna Picchu climb presents more obstacles. Once you could climb to the summit whenever you wished. Then a guard house was built and visitors started being required to sign in. Today you must buy a special ticket for climbing as well as your entry ticket to Machu Picchu; permission to climb must be secured six months in advance. But back then, you could still make a spontaneous trip.

I flew to Cusco where the streets were bright and beautiful as always. The tiled orange roofs stretched off into the distance from the Plaza de Armas. Tourists walked along, expressing obvious excitement to simply be in Perú in the midst of a great journey. I walked cobbled streets, taking in the mountain air of one of the world's great adventure cities. Then I boarded a train for that three-hour journey through the beautiful countryside: down into the valley, farther down into the rainforest, along the river; into the hidden city; and finally back to Aguas Calientes at the foot of Machu Picchu.

My perspective had changed since my last visit. Aguas Calientes survived on the influx of tourism. Its location was a charming spot nestled into a mountainous valley by a thundering river, but the village was discordant — as if it didn't really belong in this ancient place.

I hiked up to the gates and into the tiny, majestic Inca city that lured so many travelers to Perú.

I passed the sacred rock, already surrounded by diverse faith healers chanting their pathways to enlightenment and banging their heads against the stone in the morning sunlight.

Behind the sacred rock crouched the gatehouse and the stairway to the top of the mountain. It was a narrow path, sometimes no wider than a hand's width, hewn through the jungle. The trail wound up the mountain through stone and vegetation with a majestic drop on either side.

The sun was warm, the air bracing: this was a good day for a climb.

I had just begun the journey when the rains came.

Immediately, the walkway became slippery. The jungle leaves glistened as they collected the moisture on their slick, waxy surface. No rusty cables bolted into stone could keep the mountain from claiming the lives of a couple people per year. I clutched the spiky strands of the safety cable, wondering if I'd be among the dead before this afternoon ended.

Sooner or later, the hike to Wayna Picchu will be forbidden by law as too dangerous for an increasingly timid world.

But the climb wasn't illegal that day.

Up, up I went, and with every step, rain pelted me. The precipitation became ever more chilling as the temperature dropped. Jungle leaves drooped with the weight of falling water and battered me with waving stalks. Next to the path, the cliff plummeted straight down into the raging water below.

I laughed; already my adventure turned glorious: the rain, the cold, the danger.

Descending, tourists deemed me a fool for continuing upward. There was barely enough room for them to pass on the narrow walkway. I had to plaster myself against the cliff face as the water flowed down its surface, soaking my back.

"You'll be struck by lightning," one warned.

But I only cackled and struggled upward.

"That is a good way to die!" I called back.

The descending tourists shook their heads dismissively and scurried down to safety, hunched in their thousand-dollar expedition jackets bought to protect them from the elements.

I continued ever upward.

The path got worse; the mud grew deep: ankle deep, knee deep, until I struggled and sweated as I climbed, drenched inside and out, leather jacket heavy and dripping, body shaking with cold and excitement. The green rainforest spread out below and the raging water became a thin blue ribbon in the distance.

Lightning struck.

I looked down into the horseshoe-shaped cradle in which Machu Picchu dominates the epicenter. From that lofty perspective, I felt as if I might be standing upon the only safe place in the universe, as if creation had come into being for me alone. In harmony with nature, I understood my place in space and time, at long last at peace.

I felt a sudden, overwhelming confidence that everything would work out as it should.

Chapter 33

Bribing the Police

I set about beginning my sixth year in Perú. During my time at Milton School, I'd obtained a work visa; convenient because, among other benefits, this allowed me to get my own *Recibos por Honorarios* (the work papers that allowed me to get paid). However, in order to keep a work visa, you have to have a valid contract. Since I wasn't working at Milton School anymore, I was short in that category.

I phoned a friend of mine named Claudia who had her own company.

"Hey, can you use a translator on the payroll?"

"Sure, why?"

"Because I need an employment contract to keep my work visa."

"Oh, no problem. Come on down and sign one."

So I went down and signed a contract, thinking all would be fine. However, a week or so later, I received a phone call from Claudia.

"Um, the police just showed up."

"What! Why?"

"They were sent by the Department of Labor to verify your work contract."

Her words hit me like a punch in the stomach. The last thing you need is for the government to become aware of you. But the news was strange, even suspicious, since my work contract was perfectly legal.

"What did they say?"

"Well, they showed up expecting to find you at work, even though the contract hasn't been approved yet."

"Oh, we should be fine then, since I wasn't working yet."

"Yes, but they had a typed document that said I'd given you a small stipend for lunches and made me sign it."

"What?"

"Now they are threatening me with major fines for illegally offering payment to an undocumented worker."

"Are you serious?"

I was starting to freak out, but Claudia didn't seem to think this was a big problem.

"Meh, they want us to pay them something to leave us alone; that's how it's done down here. We have an appointment at the police station in a couple hours. Bring money."

"OK, I'll be there," I said, and I hung up the phone.

A lump formed in my stomach as I got dressed to meet Claudia. The most disturbing part of this situation was that I'd been attempting to do everything within the rule of law. And for that, we were being punished. In a sense, we'd already lost. Even if the police found nothing irregular in our behavior, they'd still stress us so that we wasted a day or two worrying. I'd have been really angry about the situation if I hadn't been so concerned about getting arrested.

I met Claudia, and we drove to the police station. I expected Claudia to be upset, since this irregularity started with me asking her for a favor. No one enjoys police interviews.

Instead, Claudia treated the situation as a joke. "These officers think they're more important than they are," she said.

The police station at the center of Lima sat like a giant cockroach behind a huge fence. It was a squat brown building with a rickety metal service stairway bolted to the back wall. The stairway shook alarmingly as we climbed it. At the top, we knocked on a door with a small portal in the center, and were ushered inside.

Immediately within the door were 20 desks jammed into an area designed to hold two or three at most. Claudia had said she'd met with two policemen, but only one waited for us. This policeman, a scrawny guy in a brown suit with coffee-stained cuffs, cordially offered us a seat. He got straight to business. "So," he said, "we have this document saying you've been paying this American although he has no work visa."

"Actually, I do have a work visa," I said, showing the policeman my documentation.

Producing the document caused the officer to squint and grab the rim of his glasses between his thumb and forefinger, then purse his lips and make sputtering noises. He did this for about ten minutes, while glowering, and then said, "Yes, but your current contract has not yet been validated, so you're not free to work."

"But I wasn't working."

"Ah," said the officer with a grimace, "but we have this document that says you have received payment from Señora Claudia."

"She says you typed that document and made her sign it."

The officer's glower did not change.

I realized arguing with this policeman was useless. He was expert at constructing a bogus situation in which he held all the cards. Claudia had fallen into his trap by signing the paper he wrote.

"Regarding this document . . ." the officer said, his voice trailing off for effect.

"What's going to happen?" I asked.

"Oh, we could go to trial. Trial would mean problems for Señora Claudia, probably resulting in a big fine and a lot of paperwork."

Claudia merely laughed. Apparently she still didn't consider this matter to be a serious issue. I couldn't help but wonder how often she had tangled with the police through the years. I decided to follow her lead. After all, she was the one who knew how a situation like this was commonly handled. I realized that it was ethnocentric of me to rush to assumptions. Who was I to be critical of local procedures?

"So," I asked, "what can we do to resolve this?"

That's the critical language: You never overtly suggest a bribe, but if you innocently imply you're willing to make an arrangement, the law enforcement officer takes it from there. They are professionals.

"Hmm," the officer said, his demeanor changing dramatically. "Our local football club is doing a fund raiser for new uniforms. If you'd care to make a donation to that, I could eliminate this document."

"A 'donation,'" I said.

"Yes," the officer replied. The guy looked almost sheepish.

"How much of a donation?"

The officer said nothing.

That was clever enough, I thought: good negotiators always hope you'll throw out a big number.

I weighed my options. How did I know I wasn't walking into a trap? This policeman had already invented one infraction. How could I be sure he wouldn't bust me for attempting to bribe a police official? But then I realized that if he did try to bring something like this to court, we had plenty of ammunition to fight any charges. The fact remained: I hadn't done anything illegal.

"How about S/. 100?"

"That will be fine," the officer said, looking suddenly very calm.

I started to reach into my wallet, but he stopped me.

"No, I'll just walk over there, and you can slip it under this folder on my desk," he said, pointing to his desktop. He then got up and walked off.

I looked at Claudia, who pursed her lips. "You probably went high," she said. "I think he would have taken S/. 50."

I shook my head and placed the S/. 100 bill under the folder as the officer had instructed.

He returned and tore up Claudia's signed declaration before our eyes.

"New uniforms for our football team," he said, as if we were his two best friends in the world. "Would you guys like to come out and watch the games?"

"I'll think about it," I said.

He shook our hands and escorted us to the door. I came to realize that the whole interaction had actually been very efficiently handled. The expenses incurred in both money and time were miniscule, and the local authorities had also afforded themselves an opportunity to evaluate our petition. Claudia's nonchalant attitude had proven to be justified and I resolved to interpret similar situations with greater flexibility in the future. Rigidly adhering to my preconceptions wasn't worth the stress.

Chapter 34

Locked up in a Chilean Prison

The incident with the policeman convinced me to give up my work visa and return to my previous tactic of living in Perú as an eternal tourist. Unfortunately, giving up a work visa is almost as complex as getting one in the first place. The final step involves leaving the country and reentering with a different status.

By this time, I'd found a new friend. Getting older and settling down a bit, my nights out consisted primarily of playing poker on Pizza St., where Azucena routinely took all our money. Pizza St. was a line of bars right in the center of Miraflores just off Parque Kennedy. The red brick street is closed to vehicles, and every establishment has constructed a canopy for outdoor seating. The result is a narrow walkway down the middle that becomes packed with people on weekends. There is always something interesting to see.

Playing poker was a great way to meet new expats; if the company of newcomers became intolerable, you could always concentrate on your cards. The bars didn't mind if we showed up and spilled our chips onto the table so long as we kept ordering drinks.

The most avid poker player's name was Hines, a dark-haired computer programmer who always found time to get away from his monitor and spend a few hours at the gym. He was about my age, and was one of the more stable expats I'd encountered living abroad. I found out Hines was also contemplating a trip across the border and back to renew his visa, so we decided to join forces.

"Where do you want to go, Hines, Ecuador or Chile?" I asked.

"Chile, definitely Chile," Hines replied. "The border crossing at Ecuador is a bit sketchy."

Soon enough we were on our way. We flew into Taca. I'd made the 20-hour bus-trip previously, but this time we splurged and flew to Taca by commuter plane in 59 minutes. A surprisingly large number of destinations in Perú are either an hour's flight or a 20-hour bus ride away. Generally, the flights are three times more expensive, but no one chooses the bus unless strapped for cash or looking for adventure.

When we deplaned, the taxi drivers guessed exactly why we were there.

"Hey, do you guys need a ride to Arica to attend to your visas?" a taxi driver said.

"Yup."

"Come with me, luxury taxi!"

"How much?"

"One hundred soles."

"For both of us?"

"Yes."

Hines started forward, but I stopped him.

"That means the total amount of money you receive from us is one hundred soles, right? You aren't expecting to have two hundred soles in your hand at the end of this transaction?" Payment terms must be clear in advance.

"Yes," the driver said.

"Fifty soles each?"

"Yes."

"OK," I agreed.

The taxi driver grabbed our bags and jumped in his faded white-and-Bondo-colored cab.

In my early days, I did everything cheaply. Back then, I'd take the five-sol bus to Chile. Upon arriving at the customs building at the border, the guards always glowered at me authoritatively, all a part of their act. In truth, I'd heard of no one who'd been denied entry into Chile or Perú.

Our taxi driver pulled up to the immigrations booth at the Chilean border. Hines and I unbuckled our seat belts to leave the car for the inevitable discussion with a disengaged border guard, but the driver stopped us.

"No," he said. "Give me your passports, and I'll handle it."

Hines and I looked at each other and shrugged.

The driver left the car and hobbled into the office, pushing his way past a long line of people. In less than three minutes, he emerged with exit stamps on our passports.

"Seriously?" we asked.

"No problem, no problem."

I chuckled to myself. Apparently, border control procedures are only a problem if you're broke or unconnected.

The driver pulled us up to the Chilean border post and left the car again. This time he emerged from the building in less than a minute.

"Here you go," he smiled.

I paged through my passport and found an entry stamp to Chile. I shook my head. There was something slightly creepy about entering a foreign country without even talking to a border official, but I shrugged it off.

The driver accelerated. We were on our way. I looked back and noticed a sign on the Peruvian side of the expansive desert frontier.

"Welcome to Perú, Land of Pisco!" it declared.

I laughed at the sign because Chileans enjoyed antagonizing Peruvians by erroneously declaring that Pisco originated in Chile. All the evidence clearly points to Perú as the birthplace of Pisco, including the fact that both a city and a province of Perú are called Pisco. The strongest piece of evidence, however, is that Peruvian Pisco is actually delicious, whereas the Chilean version is undrinkable kerosene.

I pointed out the sign to Hines, and he laughed appreciatively, saying, "The classic tension of any two nations that share a border."

As we made our way into Arica, the driver slowed the cab appreciably, no longer inclined to turn around to face us for idle chit-chat.

"What's going on? How come you're keeping it under a hundred kilometers per hour?"

He made a random gesture with his hand. "We're in Chile now," he said. "In Chile, I must obey the traffic laws."

I nodded.

We pulled into the Las Playas hotel.

"Do you need me to pick you up tomorrow?" the driver asked.

"Sure," we replied.

"Ok, I'll be here at nine. So that's two hundred soles you owe me, one hundred each."

I sighed and shook my head in irritation, but the driver just laughed.

"I'm kidding, one hundred."

We paid him, and he took off in a cloud of dust and Bondo fragments.

*

We kicked around Arica but couldn't find much to do. For novelty's sake, we tried the Chilean versions of the Pisco sour, but they were too foul to finish. Arica serves as a free port for Bolivia: one of the few land-locked countries in the world. However, it appeared to us that most of the action in Arica took place at sea. The city itself seemed rather sleepy, and our speculation was that the other tourists who were there had also come from Perú to renew their visas.

We made our way to the only bar with nightlife in all of Arica, arriving as its doors opened — far too early. In South America, parties never begin until midnight or later.

Nevertheless, there we were. "What are we drinking?" I asked.

"Tequila," Hines replied. "No more Chilean . . . I'm not even going to dignify that swill by calling it Pisco."

We sauntered up to the bar. In one corner, a heavily-muscled bartender in a formal shirt argued with his more casually dressed manager. They weren't quite screaming at one another, but you could feel the tension. The bartender's flat face knotted in indignation and he obviously resisted the urge to speak his mind. At last, the manager barged through a swinging door into the kitchen. Managers always leave eventually, because if they stick around for the whole shift, they might need to work.

The bartender approached us. "Can I help you?" he said, still staring with squinty eyes at the door through which his manager had gone.

"Two shots of tequila," I replied.

The bartender nodded. Still staring after the manager, he reached down for shot glasses, then changed direction and grabbed two whiskey glasses instead.

Hines and I shared a confused glance, but said nothing.

Putting the whiskey glasses on the table, the angry bartender lifted a bottle of tequila and poured, muttering under his breath indignantly, presumably about his recent fight with his manager. He began filling our whiskey glasses with tequila. In a whiskey glass, a typical tequila shot would fill the glass to one finger's height. This bartender didn't stop when the tequila reached that height, but kept pouring.

I glanced at Hines and smiled.

When the tequila hit two fingers in height, I was truly satisfied: a generous pour.

But the bartender didn't stop. At three fingers, I got nervous. A general rule of drinking is never stop a bartender from serving you — but our glasses now held a dangerous level of alcohol.

At four fingers, my covert glance at Hines contained real concern.

Finally, the bartender moved his bottle from the first glass to the second and poured again.

By the time he was done, about half the bottle had been poured into our two whiskey glasses.

We paid the bartender, tipping heavily, but he barely acknowledged us as he continued muttering and glancing at the door through which his manager had gone.

"Holy cow," Hines said.

"I don't think I can shoot all this," I replied.

We stood at the bar, gazing at our tequila shots in a state of indecision. However, you can't stand around all night sipping tequila, so we finally lifted our glasses.

"Here we are, in a foreign country, knowing no one, in a strange bar," I reminded Hines quietly. "We should keep our wits about us."

"Absolutely!" Hines replied.

Our glasses clinked.

I got about halfway through the drink before I stopped for a breath; then my gag reflex kicked in as I lifted the glass to finish, but I swallowed. Tequila poured out of the corners of my mouth, down my neck, onto my shirt.

Our empty glasses clunked on the bar.

"What do you think is going to happen now?" I asked.

"It won't be good," Hines replied, looking toward the swinging door and the angry, still-seething bartender.

*

After that, I mainly remember flashing lights, more drinks, and a blurry taxi ride back to our hotel. I awoke around seven the next morning in one of those annoying states of alertness that sometimes follow a hard night of drinking. Since I was awake, I decided to take a shower.

The shower helped. As I came out of the bathroom and started dressing, I noticed that Hines's bed was empty. I looked back in the bathroom to make sure he wasn't in there. Nothing.

I looked in the closet. No Hines. The dude was simply gone. I'd lost him.

I glanced at my watch. Our taxi driver would arrive in an hour.

I sighed, trying to recall what had happened to Hines the night before. Recollection proved impossible. The memories I could dredge up were incoherent. Trying to jog my memory only resulted in a throbbing headache.

The last clear memory I had concerned the two of us and the long pour of tequila.

"Shoot," I said aloud.

I'd probably be called upon to answer questions about Hines eventually. You can't lose somebody in a South American country and not have the authorities come knocking on your door with uncomfortable questions.

I sighed and began to pack. What else could I do? I briefly thought of throwing Hines's stuff into the garbage but didn't: I wouldn't want my fingerprints on his effects.

At 8:45 a.m. I was ready to leave, and sat down, wondering what to do next.

A loud knock made the door shiver.

That was quick! I wasn't expecting the FBI to show up until I was back in the US, working as a third-grade English teacher in a rural Wisconsin town.

"Who is it?" I asked.

"Open up: it's me — Hines."

Relief flooded me. Sure, I may have committed the world's worst party foul by leaving a drunken companion behind, but now I saw no embarrassing consequences. Hooray!

I opened the door.

Hines appeared a bit disheveled, but generally OK. Not until then did I realize he could have turned up without an eye, or with an amputated hand.

Hines stumbled in.

"Where were you?" I asked.

"I spent the night in a Chilean prison," he muttered disgustedly.

"What?"

He shook his head and started for the bathroom. "Think I have time for a shower?"

"You better take one whether we have time or not."

He nodded.

I wanted to hear the rest of the story, but it was nearly nine by then, so I went looking for our driver.

When I walked out to the lobby, the driver waited there like a guardian angel.

"Ha ha!" he said. "Looks like you had fun last night."

I thanked the universe for all reliable drivers of the world. The fact that he didn't even recoil at the sight of me testified to how much that man had experienced in his life.

"We're almost ready; my friend is in the shower," I explained.

The driver screwed up his face in a way that said, *Sure, sure, sure, I understand completely; don't worry about it, take your time, I've been in the situation you're in now on a million separate occasions and I only wish I'd had somebody comprehending like me to deal with in those instances.*

I went back to our room.

Hines had himself looking more or less normal.

"Our taxi is here."

We grabbed our stuff and left. On the long ride back to Perú, Hines had the chance to tell me the story.

"What do you remember from last night?" he asked.

"A big tequila shot and some flashing lights."

"More or less what I remember," he replied, "but I've pieced together the rest." He cleared his throat and collected himself. "I think I had a few more drinks. Then I ran out of Chilean pesos. So I left the bar and started wandering home. I didn't really know where I was or where I was going. I stopped a couple taxies and tried to get a ride, but I didn't make much sense, or was too drunk: none of them would give me a ride. Eventually, the police came." He rubbed his face. "The police picked me up and took me to the station. They threw me in a cell."

"A cell?"

"Yeah, with bars. Bars and a cot."

"Ouch."

"I just sat there trying to collect my thoughts. Finally, I began thinking I could bribe these police to let me out, but I didn't have any Chilean money. Then I remembered I had some Peruvian soles. I reached into my pocket and pulled them out. I had like three hundred."

"You had a hundred US dollars worth? That should have been enough."

"So I thought. I told the two guards, 'Hey, I'll give you three hundred Peruvian soles if you let me go.'"

"What did they say?"

"They said, 'No, this isn't Perú; you can't bribe us.'"

"Oh, no!"

"So there I sat. The hours ticked by. Every now and then I asked them to let me leave, but they'd just grunt or ignore me entirely. At about four in the morning, they brought two drunk and rowdy dudes into the next cell.

"At about eight, I said, 'Come on, guys, I need to get to Las Playas hotel because a taxi is waiting to pick me up at nine. I've been here all night.'

"'Where do you need to go?' they asked.

"'Las Playas,' I replied.

"'Do you know how to get there?'

"'Yeah, it's right around the corner.'

"At this they grunted and tossed me my passport.

"'There's the door,' one of them said. He waved and didn't even look up.

"I glanced over at the door. I was going to protest that they hadn't opened up my cell, but then I realized the cell door was already partially open. I realized that the cell had been open all night long!"

"What!" I cried, and then burst into laughter. "You spent all night in an unlocked jail cell?"

"Yup, they were waiting for me to sober up so I could get home without problems. Actually, they were pretty considerate when you think about it."

Hines avoided drinking tequila for a while after that, perhaps because he didn't want a repeat of that night, but more likely so he could continue to say, "The last time I drank tequila, I ended up in a Chilean prison."

Chapter 35

Hanging out with Alan Garcia

I got a job as an editor for a web page called *Inca Expat* which touted itself as the English-language portal to the country. *Inca Expat* had an email list that hovered around thirty thousand addresses, and the site received about a quarter of a million hits a month, so it was on the smallish side, but still big enough to be recognized. The main offices were in a black, ten story building off Avenida Jose Pardo. I only had to go in twice a week for meetings and to put together our Wednesday mass email.

My boss was a tall, blond man from Finland named Anton Hasu. Anton had a sincere affection for Perú and a good sense of humor.

Shortly before starting the job, I'd established my Perú blog, *Streets of Lima*. The web page was new, but the advertising revenue had already become a steady source of income. Anton didn't necessarily approve of me maintaining a personal blog at the same time as I worked for his web page, but I stood firm: I needed the supplementary income and the blog took less time than taking on additional private classes. Anton could understand that funds were always tight, so we made it work.

As editor of *Inca Expat*, I automatically appeared on a plethora of random mailing lists. One mailing list claimed to be managed by the Peruvian government itself. Still, I was startled to receive a very formal invitation: "President Alan Garcia personally invites you to a ceremony at the Government Palace in the center of Lima."

Whatever Alan Garcia wanted with me, this was too good an opportunity to pass up, so I printed the invitation and made my way out the door of the *Inca Expat* offices, waving to Anton as I went.

In the elevator that took me from the seventh floor to street level, I checked my pockets for the official "Press" badge that I'd made for myself using Photoshop. One of the odd little quirks of the world is that no matter how serious and intense the security in some places, folk may become more accommodating the second you show them a "Press" badge.

My badge consisted of a piece of double-sided printout from my computer that I'd laminated after signing the back. The badge displayed my photo, an offical-looking serial number I chose at random, and the ever-important large red letters spelling "Press."

Homemade press badge in hand, I boarded a *combi* and made my way to Perú's Government Palace. After an hour's ride, I stepped out of the *combi* at the Plaza Mayor in the center of Lima.

The Government Palace of Lima is an impressive structure. It's a large, cream-colored colonial style mansion built by Francisco Pizarro in 1535. The Palace is surrounded by a wrought iron fence, and the main door overlooks a courtyard between the fence and the Plaza Mayor.

When I arrived, a large crowd of real journalists milled outside a guard house in a small alley beside the Palace. Most of these journalists wore lanyards around their necks from which their press badges dangled. I had a lanyard saying *Inca Expat*, so I did the same. Most of the journalists had large, expensive-looking cameras. I had only a cell phone with a one-megapixel camera on it. This I held to my mouth as if it were a recording device, pretending to take voice notes, speaking loudly in English to augment my credibility.

In due time, a security guard with a huge, oily machine gun slung over his shoulder came to the guard house door. He looked at us from the top of a small flight of stairs and ordered those out front to form a line, gesturing to a roped off area.

The gun made me nervous, but I'd attract too much attention sprinting away down the alley, so I followed instructions and took up my position in the line.

I waited with the other twenty or so journalists.

One by one, the journalists went up to the guard. The guard wore a dark blue uniform which nicely offset the gold thread of his embroidered name and his gold badge. His pants were tucked smartly into laced black boots. He held a dot-matrix sheet with names printed on it. I noticed that, occasionally, phony journalists were turned away, no matter how big their cameras were. My mouth went dry.

Finally, the security guard glanced up and saw me. He gestured impatiently, urging me forward.

"Name?"

I gave it.

He looked at the list for a while. "I'm not finding anyone by that name."

"Maybe you need the name of my publication." I gave him this, too.

He continued to scan his list, then shook his head.

"My name must be there," I said, "I received this invitation in my email." I pulled out my printed invitation. "Oh, and here's my press badge."

He looked at my press badge, and his eyes widened.

"Oh, why didn't you say so?" he smiled, and began frantically ushering me forward, pushing others out of his way.

Hardly daring to believe my luck, I stepped forward into a small, shadowy room with dark brown walls. Light poured in through open doorways at either side of the room, creating an odd, glowing effect. There was a metal detector set up in front of the opposing doorway. Two more security guards in blue uniforms sat beside a collapsible table. I was certain I'd be discovered at this next level of security. One of the guards regarded me lazily and pointed at the detector.

I stepped through.

My passage set off a series of sirens and alarms.

"Oh, I forgot to take off my belt," I said, expecting to be tackled, but the guard wasn't concerned. He only yawned and waved me onward, not insisting on so much as a pat down.

I went where the guard pointed and found myself emerging into the courtyard between the Government Palace and the perimeter fence. Here there were several attractive women dressed in red uniforms who smiled widely and directed the new arrivals toward some aluminum bleachers set up in a prominent position beside the courtyard. I could see the journalists with their large cameras were taking their positions on the bleachers, so I walked over and climbed on as well.

We waited for a while, and then a hush descended over the proceedings. Glancing to my right, I could see a crowd of people had gathered in the Plaza Mayor outside the perimeter fence. I looked back to the massive ceremonial doors of the Government Palace. Two guards stood beside the doors wearing red jackets with blue frills, gold buttons, and blue pants that matched the frills. In their white-gloved hands they clutched ornamental flag poles topped with the Peruvian flag.

The doors opened to absolute silence. Ten men and one woman emerged through the door onto a flight of red-carpeted steps. They were dressed in navy blue or gray suits. The woman was dressed in an elegant burgundy dress. One of the men had a rainbow-colored sash across his chest. They all took their places on the red carpet in front of the Palace so as to face the courtyard.

Last to emerge was Alan Garcia, the President of Perú himself. Garcia towered over all the other members of the assembly. He was a powerfully built, attractive man with black hair. He waved and smiled to a round of applause, then crossed his hands in front of his waist and settled in to watch.

There I was, standing within ten yards of the President. I became suddenly fearful that my mere presence could create some sort of international incident. I hunched down and tried to make myself as innocuous as possible.

Music began to play and we were treated to a series of performances by gifted dance troupes. They ran out from a staging area behind our bleachers and began dancing on a large red carpet that had been rolled out in the courtyard. The costumes were amazing. Bright red and green and blue clad dancers whirled and spun through a series of dizzying routines before my eyes. I came to learn that this event was the launch of the *Inti Raymi* festival in Cusco. The troupes were giving a preview of what was in store at the upcoming celebration.

In the press box, I began to sense the hard-working, legitimate journalists were wondering who I was and what competitor had dispatched me. Luckily, most were too busy with their camera bags and high-tech equipment to ask any questions.

Every few minutes, I took a few blurry, one-megapixel shots with my cell phone for later publication. My camera made a pig-like squeal when it captured images, in stark contrast to the expensive purr of rapid-fire DSLRs with six-inch lenses. Inevitably, my batteries drained; then I simply stood there, shuffling my feet. I even tried to recreate my phone's shutter noise by blowing air behind my teeth, but that made people swivel their heads to glare at me, so I stopped. Having come so far, I didn't want to be found out now. Before the ceremony ended, I slipped toward the door I'd come in by, retracing my steps.

On the way out, Alan Garcia caught my eye and seemed to give me a diplomatic nod. The nod might have just been a coincidental shift in body position, but it seemed to convey all of his importance and responsibility as a head of state. Thoroughly outclassed, I made my way into the street and caught a *combi* home.

Chapter 36

Gourmet-Restaurant Reviewer

Part of my job with *Inca Expat* included arranging and attending promotions of gourmet restaurants. Over the previous decade in Perú, gourmet restaurants had sprouted until Lima gained renown as a premier South American gastronomic destination.

Inca Expat loved finding new restaurants to promote. We'd call the owner, asking to visit, sample the food, and take pictures. Then we'd do a write up for our weekly newsletter which would generate a fair amount of business for the restaurant. This was a popular feature among those of us who worked at *Inca Expat*, who didn't make enough money to dine at such restaurants otherwise.

One Thursday afternoon, I took a taxi to a restaurant whose owner had contacted me. I'd written down the address, but when I arrived at the indicated street number, no restaurant stood there, only a private residence with a dark wooden door. The door was framed by a white wall with a couple of large, thick-stemmed green bushes. The center of the door had a small portal covered with a couple of bars for security.

Scratching my head and hoping I hadn't misheard the street name, I left my taxi and rang the doorbell.

"Hello?" came a voice of the sort you'd hear from a private residence.

That was weird.

"Hi, I'm here with *Inca Expat* to do a restaurant promotion."

The portal behind the bars swung open and I found myself regarding a pair of wizened eyes, although the lattice of bars made it difficult to see much.

"Oh yes!" the voice replied, the eyes widening in excitement as I flashed my press badge. The wooden door opened to reveal the lobby of a bustling restaurant. Behind a row of elegant windows hidden by the white, street-side wall, I saw a series of tables draped with cream-colored cloths and adorned with flowers in vases. I stepped through the open door onto a pathway of varnished stone.

"Hello, my friend," said a graying man with a jovial air. He wore a smart white shirt with the top two buttons open, a common South American practice. Black dress pants and expensive looking shoes completed the ensemble. "My name is Ricardo, and I am your host."

He led me to a table where he immediately served me a Pisco sour. Most restaurants I was promoting started off by giving me a Pisco sour: a few drinks always enhance your appreciation of a restaurant.

Ricardo told me the history of his establishment as I took diligent notes, but truly I couldn't concentrate on his words. The night before I'd received a call from my old friend Kyle, announcing his return to Perú for a quick visit. Since I hadn't seen Kyle for five years, we stayed out late exchanging stories over pitchers of beer. My stomach remained unsettled as Ricardo brought out my first entree.

"Oysters!" he said with a smile. "Have you ever tried oysters?"

I admitted I hadn't, and tried ignoring my stomach's warnings about raw oysters. I didn't want to embarrass myself by being sick here.

Ricardo set the jiggling plate of oysters down in front of me. I snapped pictures for my article, then lifted a shell. I gulped the oyster and it plummeted down my throat.

That raw oyster went down easy. Too easy.

My stomach decided it would be just as easy for the oyster to come back up as it had been for me to swallow it down.

"What else do you have?" I asked. I needed to put less challenging food on top of the oyster, to hold it in place.

Ricardo laughed and slapped me on the back, mistaking my discomfort for enthusiasm. He proceeded to call for seven different gourmet plates from the restaurant. I finished off my Pisco sour, took my photos, and gorged myself on the excellent food.

Ricardo called for bottles of wine and repeatedly filled my glass.

"I knew I'd be friends with you after I saw you handle that Pisco sour," he laughed. "I never trust a man who doesn't drink!"

Three hours later, our table was littered with the leftovers of a dozen plates and three empty bottles of wine. I sensed a lull. "Is that everything you wanted to show me?"

"Naw, let's just take a break for an hour or so, and then we can start a second round."

I exhaled, not sure if I could meet his challenge, but willing to try.

We had a quick tea before the next round of food began. By then the wine had loosened Ricardo's tongue, and the waiters and waitresses were chuckling. Ricardo called one of them over and whispered into his ear. A few minutes later, a champagne glass arrived, containing a glowing green liquid.

"This is what they drink in Spain after a meal," Ricardo said.

"Ah."

I drank it, to Ricardo's delight.

After a moment of reflection, a warm sensation emanated from my stomach.

"Come on, let me drive you home," he said.

I had severe doubts that the guy could even stand up, much less drive.

"Naw," I said. "I think I'll want a taxi."

"Come on," Ricardo continued, "you can trust me. I'm an excellent drunk driver. The secret is to go very slow and not make abrupt movements."

I eventually convinced Ricardo that I didn't want to impose upon him for a ride. Eventually, I made my way home, where I slept until about noon the next day.

To some, this line of work may be a dream job, but eating so much gourmet food caused me to gain a considerable amount of weight.

Chapter 37

Hiking the Inca Trail with Two Olympians

At the peak of my glorious but unhealthy restaurant-reviewing lifestyle, I received a call from Roberto Carcelen.

Roberto is a cross-country skier who became Perú's first winter Olympian after representing the country at Vancouver and then again at Sochi. He also ran a business guiding people down the Inca Trail, called "Inca Runners." The Inca Trail is one of Perú's foremost tourist draws, a network of trails running throughout the Andes on which the Incas traveled between their various cities. The views are spectacular: hiking the trail allows access to ruins inaccessible otherwise.

When I'd interviewed Roberto for *Inca Expat*, we'd immediately clicked, since I too have a background in cross-country skiing, a sport uncommon in Perú. Both Roberto and I enjoyed meeting someone with similar experience.

"Hey," Roberto said on the phone, "what kind of shape are you in?"

"Terrible," I replied. For the record, that's always the smart answer when speaking to Olympic athletes.

"Nonsense, you're a former cross-country skier: you can handle anything! We'll be doing the Inca Trail in a few months. Want to join us?"

"What route?"

"The hard one, from Choquequirao to Machu Picchu."

Despite my misgivings about my fitness, I couldn't pass up this opportunity. Choquequirao is a set of ruins purportedly as large and spectacular as Machu Picchu, but almost free of tourists since it can be reached only by a strenuous 20-mile hike. "Yeah, I'm in."

"Excellent!" Roberto said.

I hung up the phone and went jogging. I'd need to be as fit as I could get.

*

Only three of us were slated for the expedition: myself, Roberto, and another cross-country skier named Martin Koukal from the Czech Republic, a bronze medalist at the Vancouver Olympics and gold medalist at the 2003 world championships. Martin was famous, and not just for his exploits as a cross-country skier: He had also climbed Cho Oyu in Nepal, the sixth-highest mountain in the world, without oxygen canisters or *sherpa* guides.

At an early lunch, Martin mentioned that he'd quit the Czech national team to race for a professional

European squad. From his description, the money was better, but he didn't seem like a person who'd settle for less than Olympic or World Cup gold. Although he spoke of rejoining the national team for the next calendar year, something in his demeanor suggested a concern that his window of opportunity might now be closed.

I found his situation fascinating. Here was a man who had followed an unconventional life path to actually become the best in the world at his chosen pursuit. But even with this achievement, he faced outside pressures and difficult choices. I marveled at the way conformity pressured people toward conventional lifestyles — no matter how unsatisfying or unrewarding that lifestyle might be. Even becoming a World Champion did not spare you from social pressure.

I soon developed a deep respect for Martin, who was an intense fellow who'd accelerate during a simple walk down a street, as if fearing you'd pass him. I found this amusing: I was clearly no physical threat, but after a few decades of the intense competition of the World Cup, a person develops habits.

Then again, perhaps to become a world champion, you must perceive everyone as a threat.

Envisioning an Olympic athlete, people imagine a person who takes diligent, almost obsessive care of his or her body. Although this was true with Martin, the guy also loved his beer. When we first went out to eat, I asked him if he was allowed to drink, considering what I assumed was his stringent nutritional regimen.

"Of course I drink," he said. "American athletes always avoid beer; these concerns are absolutely ridiculous."

I smiled, thinking that Martin had just thrown down the wrong gauntlet, and decided to have a little fun. "Then I challenge you to a drinking contest," I said. "Can you drink all night and still go running tomorrow?"

Martin looked at me with a flicker of affection on his craggy face: his lips quivered in a barely perceptible smile. "I am a professional," he stated simply, meaning that our drinking contest was definitely on.

This happened two days before our scheduled hike over the strenuous path from Cachora to Choquequirao. A drinking contest wasn't a good idea, but knowing I was doing something stupid had never stopped me before.

Martin selected Finlandia Vodka, and we began the match at just past eleven. I wasn't expecting to match Martin Koukal shot for shot all night long. Observing him jogging around Cusco's Plaza de Armas had shown me that he was a physical marvel.

But I had a trump card to play. When you meet people from other countries, they commonly disparage the US. Most of the time, after talking with people from various places, they'll admit that their preconceptions about Americans are wrong, that they have nothing against the US. However, such moments of understanding take time to achieve.

Martin didn't know that we'd begun our drinking contest on the evening of July 3rd, and as Koukal slammed his eighth shot, the clock on the wall struck midnight.

"Happy 4th of July!" I hollered, slapping him on the back. "It's American Independence Day!" I continued, in case he didn't know. "Thanks for drinking that shot in celebration, Martin!"

Martin nearly coughed up his vodka. This ended our drinking competition, as Martin then left, grumbling about "sneaky" Americans.

Still, Martin had the last laugh. The next day in the car from Cusco to the provincial town of Cachora, I was pretty much ruined. Martin looked as if he could win six races and still have enough left over to wrestle a grizzly bear.

Chapter 38

A 20-Mile Hike

At Cachora we stayed at the simple house of our *porteros*, the guys who ran the donkey train carrying our bags. The house was made of dried clay bricks. A herd of guinea pigs scurried across its dirt floor. In Perú, guinea pigs are called *cuy*, and roast *cuy* is a delicacy.

Three *porteros* would accompany us on our six-day hike to Machu Picchu. Martin and Roberto expected to run the entire distance. I would leave early in the morning and walk.

The next day I awoke early, to find myself paired with the cook, whose name was Jesus, pronounced "Hey Zeus." I was reminded of a deity every time I spoke to him. Jesus was a small man, less than 130 pounds, but watching him toss heavy bundles onto the backs of the pack donkeys convinced me of his strength.

Roberto handed me a radio to clip on my belt. I suspected the radio wouldn't work well or would probably crackle annoyingly throughout the hike. I also carried a DSLR as well as a smaller, emergency camera to help me document our journey for publication in *Inca Expat* and elsewhere.

"Hello, Jesus," I said in the morning as I prepared to set off.

Jesus smiled back at me without speaking.

"Well, which way is the trail?"

Jesus just pointed toward the mountains.

"Ok, let's go!"

The first hundred yards of our journey sloped downhill. Then the pitch turned upward, and the terrain became difficult enough to stymie a mountain goat.

On the outskirts of Cachora, the Inca Trail was still in regular use. The local people had widened and surfaced the trail with gravel so the path was level, well-drained, and solid.

When people talk about the Inca Trail, they usually mean the route from Cusco to Machu Picchu. Although that's the most famous, it's not the only trail created by Incas through the Andes. A series of ancient trails exist and, once you get into the mountains, there is a high probability that many of the pathways you find were established by the Incas.

The first trail day dawned sunny. I left about an hour earlier than Martin and Roberto. However, before I'd made any notable progress on the day's hike, the two Olympians came jogging around a corner.

"Hello!" they called happily.

I whipped out my DSLR and took their photos.

After a moment of chatting, Martin and Roberto went sprinting off up the mountain.

I sighed. It was going to be a long day.

The first 13 miles of the journey were predominantly flat. Along the way I was passed by our 80-year-old *portero*, dragging his reluctant donkey behind him.

"Great job!" he said to me, lifting his wrinkled thumb in support. He then went sprinting around the corner twice as fast as I could go.

I sighed. *Well, at least I'm out here*, I thought, plodding onward.

At mile 13, I saw a raging river to be crossed by way of a flimsy suspension bridge. I looked down with concern through the four-inch-wide spaces between its planks. The white water boiled below, rushing incredibly fast through a series of sharp and jagged boulders.

"Don't worry," Jesus said. "It's safe."

He began jumping up and down on a rotted plank that wheezed and groaned beneath his weight.

"Please stop that, Jesus," I managed to say.

Jesus smiled and scampered across the bridge, which visibly bounced and bowed under his weight. I weighed almost twice as much as Jesus.

The trick to crossing an Indiana Jones-style suspension bridge is to never look down. Of course, this is impossible, because you must ensure that your feet connect with planks not rotten to the core.

I looked down. I looked round. There was no other way across this gorge but the bridge.

The river continued to rage. I took step after shaky step, until suddenly Jesus was tapping me on the shoulder.

"You've done it!"

I looked up to see a nearly vertical wall before me.

"What's that?"

"That's the trail; the next seven miles are straight up."

I shook my head, hoisted my pack, and began climbing.

The climb was long, hard, and hot. The sun beat down on Jesus and me. I worried about how much water remained in my hydration pack. Just as I realized I'd need to ration my remaining liquid, Jesus trotted over.

"Hey, do you think I could have a drink?"

How could I say no? As far as I knew, the guy hadn't had any water all day. I offered him the little plastic hose.

Jesus took a series of tremendous gulps. "Thanks!" he said, and then turned to sprint out of sight around the next bend.

I shook my head. At least my pack was a bit lighter.

Up and up and up went the trail. Occasionally, trees arched over us, keeping the sun out of my face; but most of the trail provided no cover. I was sunburned and miserable, on a trail now so steep that my progress was agonizingly difficult and slow. However,

I was excited about being there. Joy can be found in misery, as long as there's a good view.

Now and again my radio crackled and Roberto's voice provided me assurances that he and Martin were effortlessly floating up the cliff like leaves lifted on a summer breeze.

Finally, the trail broke into a little clearing. Standing in the center of the clearing was a little hut which had been thrown together out of jungle materials. The corner posts were uneven logs stripped of their bark. Horizontal branches had been lashed to the logs to create a roof, and this had been thatched with leaves. A woman sat in the hut next to a collection of bottles. A painted wooden sign sat at the edge of the clearing: "Welcome to Santa Rosa," it said. "We have food, beer, and water."

Saved! I could replenish my scant supply of water. "How much is a liter of water?" I asked. I feared airport-terminal prices, or worse, but I didn't have a choice.

"S/. 10!" the woman responded.

I tried not to show my relief. The woman's prices, about three times normal, were reasonable in the situation. If she'd wanted $50 for a liter of water, I'd have paid it gladly.

I got out my coins and bought a bottle for Jesus as well, who was grateful.

I drank as much as I could hold, then filled my water reservoir and continued on my way with Jesus.

Hours rolled by until my radio next crackled with Roberto's voice: "Hey! Where are you?"

"I'm climbing."

"Did you get to Santa Rosa?"

"Yes."

"Well, the campground is only seventeen more switchbacks from Santa Rosa."

"Uh-huh."

I didn't believe him but started counting anyway. When I got to 25 switchbacks with the campground nowhere in sight, I stopped counting.

My stomach started rumbling, so I sat down and fumbled in my pack.

Before I'd left Cusco, I'd bought a 24-pack of Snickers candy bars. When doing anything athletic, it's not smart to let others control your access to food.

Before leaving, Roberto had kindly supplied me with a lunch comprised of a single grain of rice, a raisin, and a peanut. Roberto wanted to lose some weight to prepare for his World Cup races, so we were all on his diet. The lighter you are, the faster you go. Roberto's goal was to become utterly without mass so that he could achieve the speed of light. I harbored no such ambitions, so I hunkered down and ate a couple Snickers bars.

After an hour's break, I stood up, walked a hundred yards, and found myself at the first campsite.

"Hey," Roberto said, "you're not swearing at me!"

"Why do you say that?"

"Because most of the other people who make this trip swear at me after the first day."

Seeing me, Martin approached. He'd been doing pull-ups because the 20-mile hike wasn't strenuous enough for him.

"What did you think of that suspension bridge?" I asked him.

"No big deal."

"Weren't you afraid you'd fall through?"

"Naw," he shrugged. "If it's strong enough to hold donkeys, it's strong enough to hold us."

"Yeah," I replied, "but donkeys have four legs. If one breaks through it's still got three on the bridge. If one of ours breaks through, we're likely to fall, and if we fall . . ."

"Smashed like potato," Martin said solemnly in his thick Czech accent before wandering off.

That's when I realized Martin had a good sense of humor.

Chapter 39

Choquequirao

That night I realized my feet were in bad shape. We'd been sponsored by a running-shoe company. Although I'd worn my complimentary pair around Lima prior to the trip, I hadn't had time to ensure the shoes were properly broken in.

Nor do you find the same type of terrain in Lima that you encounter in the Andes. The downhills had done me in. I wasn't accustomed to steep gradients descending into valleys. As a result, I had identical two-inch blisters on the outside of each heel.

We all had private tents. I was sitting in the doorway of mine, picking at my feet, when Roberto came over.

"Oh, that looks pretty bad," he said.

"Do you have a needle?"

"I'll ask Martin."

Martin had one. Due to the commotion, he came over to take a look. As usual, two massive blisters weren't enough to impress the world champion.

"Now you know, the only reason you got blisters is because you didn't properly prepare your feet," he scolded me.

"Yes, you're right," I said. "I didn't wear my double-layer socks this morning."

"What you need to do," Martin continued, "is rip off the dead skin."

"You want me to rip the skin off and leave the tender part exposed?"

"Yes."

Normally I did what Martin directed without protest, but in this instance, I wasn't prepared to submit myself to the torture he suggested. I wouldn't maim my feet. "No, I'm not going to do that," I stated flatly, in a tone that brooked no argument. I then proceeded to drain the blisters.

When I finished, I curled up in my tent and hoped that my feet would heal, although I knew that one night's sleep wouldn't be enough time for that.

*

The next morning, I was shocked to see the ruins of Choquequirao from my tent. I'd been too tired from the day's hike to notice them the night before. In the morning light, the view was breathtaking. Our little yellow tents were pitched on a small clearing on the edge of a cliff face. The mountain dropped down into a valley below. On the opposing hill, there were two or three lonely lights flickering amongst the green foliage. Their sparsity made the mountain seem even more devoid of people than if there had been no lights at all, for they gave perspective as to the uninhabited space.

Choquequirao sat farther up the road on a ridge that jutted out into the valley. A mist surrounded the site, and the gray clouds were a perfect complement to the stone walls and jungle leaves. From my vantage point, I could make out some structures, but it was difficult to tell what I was looking at. There appeared to be approximately three building groups: a central plaza, a higher group behind that, and a flat promontory at the end that I guessed had valley views from every angle. Below the main structures on the top of the ridge, buildings and stairs could be seen descending down the wall. My aches and pains faded instantly away as I became excited about the prospect of exploration.

I packed my things and left camp before Martin and Roberto, who pointed me in the right direction. We were so close to the ruins that I was allowed to walk alone, without Jesus there to accompany me.

"Where's Martin?" I asked.

"He's still asleep. He doesn't wake up early."

Running out of daylight wasn't an issue for Martin. In his role of superhero, he could fly over the mountains if he wished.

Roberto said he felt ill that morning and elected to hike only as far as our campsite near the entry gate to Choquequirao. I'd awakened with a sore throat and developed a cough, but I wasn't going to miss seeing these ruins. I adjusted my small pack and hiked onward about three miles to the ruins, along narrow and difficult trails. The previous night's camp had been pitched on a ridge near the edge of a small settlement consisting of four farm houses and a couple of fenced-in areas.

I was amazed to see that people lived year round in the silent shadow of the ruined city of Choquequirao. Had it been me, I would have lived within the ruins. Who knows? Maybe they had tried and been ejected by ghosts or bureaucrats or both.

On the road, I came upon a gate house, a stone structure with a man inside. The man looked like a local, but wore a semi-official-looking vest.

"Heading to Choquequirao?" he asked.

"Yes."

"That'll be S/. 40."

"I wasn't aware that there was a fee for getting into Choquequirao."

"There is."

He sat there sternly, staring in my general direction but not making eye contact. I wasn't quite sure whether he was a legitimate government agent or a local who figured he could make a quick buck by charging a bogus entry fee. Eventually, I got out the money.

He thanked me and gave me an official-looking ticket that suggested he might have been legitimate, although anyone could hike into Cachora and have tickets printed.

"Make sure you see the llamas around the back," he said.

"Llamas?"

"Yeah, at the wall on the back side of Choquequirao you'll see images of white llamas made with stone."

"Oh."

I turned around to leave but on impulse swung back with my camera to snap a shot of the gatekeeper. Seeing the camera, he flung himself to the floor behind the counter. "No photos! No photos!"

Surprised, I shrugged and put my camera away, making one more entry in the "illegitimate" column on my mental list.

*

I limped, continuing up the trail. My blisters hurt; my sore throat hurt. Nevertheless, I found my excitement growing with every step. Here the trail was little more than a muddy rut that weaved through the wet, waxy leaves. The air was thick and humid; the morning temperature remained cool. To my left, the cliff dropped away into the valley, and with each step the mysterious ruins in the distance grew larger.

The ridge loomed larger and larger, and my vantage point shifted so that I could no longer see the principal ruins on the top. The section on the wall, which had appeared as little more than an inconsequential patch from our campsite, suddenly loomed as a complex and massive lattice of terrain transformed for terrace farming. As the morning sun continued to rise over the mountain behind me, the shadow of the peak descended into the valley. The mammoth, indomitable darkness of the shadow was titanic enough to offer a suggestive glimpse of the Earth's inevitable, timeless spin. It's humbling to find oneself in a place where even miniscule fragments of the universal forces that bind our lives are revealed. Time was represented by the ruins, and space was represented by the shadow. It was as if the heavenly bodies of our solar system conspired to caress this majestic, rolling valley.

I continued on along the path and came to a nondescript blue sign with white letters. *"Choq'ekiraw,"* it said, in what I assumed must be the spelling from the local language: *Quetcha*.

No fireworks or hoopla or confetti. No greeting but a rustle of leaves being jostled by the wind.

I recalled my first visit to Machu Picchu, before the ruins were named one of the "Seven Wonders of the World." Before Machu Picchu became a popular tourist destination, when you could think of it as your special, secret place.

Here I walked in, alone, along a stone terrace with a high wall to my right. I had climbed up now, up from the darkness, and the sun's heat could be felt in the morning light. The stones were almost yellow and moss grew from between the cracks. The occasional flower popped up along the way. The path was made of stone now, and it was flat and smooth despite years of settling.

The sense of solitude was astounding.

Here crowded no throngs of people.

Here walked only me. I felt more the explorer than ever. My discoveries might not be new to the world, but they were new to me. That was enough.

I hiked across the terrace and over the central plaza, sitting often, absorbing the ambiance of the place. The central plaza was smaller than what can be found at Machu Picchu, but it is perhaps more open with a farther reaching view.

A path wound beside a set of buildings and I walked up, up, up until I reached the flat-topped plateau I had seen from our campsite. The grass was short, and in the center there was a stack of stones with a pink flower growing out of them. The plateau overlooked the valley on three of the site's four sides. The descending walls seemed impossibly steep, dropping away beneath my feet through the clouds and down to the rushing water that carved a blue line like a pen stroke on the valley floor below. The fourth view gave me a new and different perspective on the ruins. Walls and buildings spread out along the ridge leading back up the mountain. From this vantage point I could see a dozen more places I wished to explore, though I was hesitant to abandon my current position.

I eventually continued, retracing my steps back to the central plaza to climb over another wall. I found another path, this one leading down again through the jungle. This was on the far side of the ruins, the side I hadn't been able to see on my approach. I continued on the winding path through the green leaves and the shadows, to another set of terraces that had been decorated with images of white stone llamas embedded into the walls just as the gatekeeper had said. Continuing on, I came to a small, flat observation point that allowed me to see all the llamas in one view. From there I could see that they had been placed in two diagonal lines, as if they were eternally marching upward in the hope of grazing on the green grass of the plaza.

On the way back up the stairs and switchbacks, I ran into Martin.

"Hey," I said happily.

Martin grinned broadly. He wore shorts and a lightweight running shirt. A sheen of sweat glistened on his forehead.

"I've been down to the lower ruins, plus over the top already," he said.

I nodded, but I hadn't had time to explore all that yet. The day was already growing long and I feared I wouldn't have time to see everything.

"I also ran up the trail where we're going to go tomorrow, just to have a look," he continued.

I shook my head: the guy was a marvel. "Have you had time to stop and take any pictures?" I asked. "What do you think of this place?"

He took a quick look around and then shrugged. "Bunch of rocks. I'm here for the training. See you!" The ruins hadn't reached him with their mysterious beauty: he had his mind on other things, at least, that's what he claimed. With that, he was off.

I was bemused by this example of the dedication necessary to become a world champion. I also reflected that beneath Martin's cavalier attitude lurked someone who'd spent the day going over every single inch of the ruins.

I think the place impressed him more than he wanted to let on; maybe he associated awe with weakness.

I continued my exploration, reluctantly taking my leave when the light began to fade. I reunited with Martin and Roberto at our new campsite at the foot of the ruins, exhausted but content on many levels.

Chapter 40

The Yanama Pass

Back at the tent, I peeled off my socks and shoes to see today's damage to my feet. This crop of blisters rose as big and as nasty as the last. I again drained the fluid from them before lying down to rest.

A couple hours later, Roberto shook my tent. "How are you feeling?" he asked.

"Great!" I said. I then started coughing like a madman, which damped my enthusiasm. "How about you?"

"Pretty bad," he replied. "I'm thinking that maybe we should go back."

I thought about leaving. Ahead yet lay several days of hiking and two mountain passes. Going back would certainly be easier, but I didn't like the sound of it.

"What does Martin think?"

"Martin would be disappointed."

We considered our situation jointly in silence for a time. It didn't take me long to realize that I wanted to stay even if it would kill me. "I think we should keep going," I offered.

"Are you going to be OK with your cold and those blisters?"

"Yup," I declared. Secretly I doubted it, but I couldn't give up — not yet.

*

We continued our journey.

Roberto projected that the days would get steadily easier, so I headed out in high spirits. However, I found the third day tougher than the first, and the fourth harder than the third.

Every evening I dressed my blisters, grown to the size of kiwi fruit on my feet. Martin usually stopped by to appraise them. He no longer scolded me about allowing them to develop.

I think he'd worried I would complain throughout the trip, becoming a nuisance. But one of the quirks in my personality is that when I really feel miserable, I get giggly.

I got used to my routine of draining my blisters and taping them up before each day's hike.

On the fourth day, we crossed the Veronica Pass, at an elevation of 14,000 feet. Condors spiraled in the air above us, soaring in lazy arcs.

"Hey, you made it," Roberto said as I stumbled into camp that evening.

"Yep."

"Don't worry, tomorrow is easier."

"You keep saying that, but it's never true."

*

On the fifth day, we had to cross the Yanama Pass at an elevation of 16,000 feet.

This crossing most certainly was not "easier."

Altitude has strange effects on the human body. Some say that your level of fitness is irrelevant.

Martin told us a story of one of his friends who developed pulmonary edema on an expedition in the Himalayas. Like Martin, the friend was an Olympian, but had to be carried off the mountain after only a single day's hike. He survived the ordeal, but witnessing it had clearly disconcerted Martin.

After listening to several such stories, I wasn't taking any chances. As I approached the Yanama Pass, I took no more than fifty steps at a time and then stopped, whether or not I felt tired. The trick with altitude is not to overexert, since if you become short of breath, you may never catch that breath again.

Fifty steps, rest. Fifty steps, rest.

When I hit the snow line, life became surreal for me.

At that altitude, although the whole world appears stretched out before you, it may simultaneously feel as if invisible walls are closing in: an infinite view coupled with the knowledge that you can't move fast or easily, that you're weak. If a storm should blow in, you won't be able to outrun it — not that anyone could ever outrun any storm on foot.

Climbing a daunting pass brings a sequence of disappointed hopes: at every turn along the way, you hope to see the end of the climb; as you arrive at each turn, you discover only that another twisting, challenging ascent awaits you. Crushing blow follows crushing blow, until you don't care anymore.

Then, and only then, does your final destination reveal itself. When I finally emerged at the top of the Yanama Pass, I felt a surge of emotion.

I stood for a moment at the high point of my journey and looked backward and forward. The view was equally spectacular in both directions. I found myself thinking of various students from places I'd taught through the years, wondering whether or not the advice I'd given them had been useful.

On that pinnacle, I realized that, when discussing decision-making, people tend to leave out significant points, the most important being this: Every choice has a consequence; some are good; some are bad; some are positive, but yet represent missed opportunities.

Some choices are magnificent. Very rarely, however, is a choice either "right" or "wrong."

No person can make predictions with any certainty, but naysayers will always be present on the sidelines, critical of decisions, spreading fear and doubt where none is warranted. No matter how many mistakes you make, a path to the top is always preserved. I hoped I'd conveyed that knowledge when I'd had opportunities to teach — now the only thing that remained was to convince myself.

My students' choices had always been out of my hands and remained so. I wished them, and whoever I'd influenced in my life, good luck.

Then I pushed my reflections aside and began my descent. On the way down, I crossed paths with a solitary young Andean woman riding a donkey. She looked at me kindly as I pressed myself against the wall to allow her donkey room to pass. She rode slowly by, unconcerned that her mount teetered on the edge of a 1,000-foot drop. Then she and the donkey turned the corner, disappearing as if they'd never existed.

Five hours later, as I approached our camp, Martin came to meet me. Having finished his hike early that morning, he was enjoying an evening jog. I was flattered he'd come to see me in, but concerned that I'd need to keep pace with him over these last few miles to the campsite.

"You know," he said, "I was talking to Roberto, and he said that on a normal trip you'd be one of the strongest hikers."

I smiled to hide a grimace, struggling to keep up.

"You really shouldn't compare yourself to me," he said matter-of-factly. "After all, I'm a full-time athlete. This is my job."

I hadn't been under any illusions about comparing myself to Martin Koukal, but his words were still encouraging to hear. I grunted in response.

"I think you're a pretty tough guy," Martin continued gruffly.

From a guy who referred to Choquequirao as "a bunch of rocks," this was poetry.

"You'd probably feel better on trips like this if you lost a little weight," Martin continued.

There went that buzz.

Chapter 41

Return to Machu Picchu

That night we slept at altitude with a cloudless sky; it got very cold. Shortly before bed, Roberto and I sat by the fire rifling through the first-aid kit, trying to find something to help us fight our pains and the cold. We were hoping for morphine, but we'd take anything we could get.

"Wait a minute," Roberto cried. "I think I have something."

I looked over, expecting to see a dripping syringe. Instead, he held up an orange plastic packet.

"What is that?"

"A set of chemical hand-warmers," Roberto said.

I saw his logic. Our fancy sleeping bags would trap and reflect body heat. Any kind of heating element contained inside them would greatly increase their efficiency.

"But there are only two," I said. "What about Martin?"

We glanced around, but Martin was nowhere to be seen.

"Aw, that guy's superhuman. He'll be fine."

Hand-warmer clutched in my fist, I stumbled back to my tent. The short walk in the cold, combined with my not inconsiderable exhaustion, made my hands shake so hard I could barely zip the tent closed.

A short while later I was lying on my back inside my sleeping bag with my hand-warmer pressed firmly against my chest. Heat spilled over me like molten wax. I slept like a baby.

*

The next morning, we got close enough to civilization that we could actually catch a bus down to Hydrolico. Hydrolico is an electrical station behind Machu Picchu, where we could ride a train that travels to Aguas Calientes.

We hoped to catch the train, so Roberto urged the bus driver to hurry.

The driver responded with a salute and floored the accelerator of his rickety bus.

"The road we're driving on," Roberto said, "was part of the Inca Trail a few years ago. In these sections they widened the trail with bulldozers to allow vehicles to use it."

The bus rattled recklessly around blind corners. Sitting in the back on the driver's side, I had a clear view of the valley floor, at the bottom of a sheer drop. I tried not to look at it, but my eyes kept getting pulled in that direction. Up ahead, you could see the path carved out of the mountain wall. In the distance, I clearly saw wash-outs and oncoming vehicles.

"Hey, Roberto, is there room enough for an oncoming vehicle to pass?"

"Yes, there are passing sections."

"But what if . . ."

My words were cut off as the driver slammed on his brakes, sending the bus into a skid. Directly in front of us, another bus also skidded to a halt. The two drivers gesticulated at each other in silence through their dingy windshields. Finally, they agreed on a procedure to attempt to inch by each other.

As the two buses passed side by side on the one-lane road, my eyes stayed glued to the window and the paralyzing drop that seemed my imminent destination.

Rocks were falling into the ravine, dislodged by our vehicle's tires.

I counted the seconds it took for those falling rocks to hit the ground as they dropped down into the valley. I couldn't get an accurate count because they never seemed to hit, they just kept falling perpetually.

"I am reminded of the Himalayas," Martin said pleasantly. "But on a road like this in the Himalayas, you see the burned-out wreckage from lots of crashed cars down below."

We finally made it past the other bus, but by then my nerves were frayed. Roberto's, too.

"Señor, it's OK if we don't make the train. Take your time," Roberto said.

Not even Martin protested.

*

We did miss the train, which meant we hiked a final three mile trip to reach Aguas Calientes.

Civilization felt strange, closing around me after the solitude of the Andes. Tourists flooded the streets in red and yellow clothing they had purchased from street vendors. They spoke loudly in a polyglot of languages.

I called Azucena to say I'd survived the trip. Then all three of us made our way to the hotel where we'd reserved a room for three, and I dove into the shower.

A hot shower: the one advantage civilization had over the trail. Everything else was a downgrade.

The day we arrived happened to be the 100-year celebration of Hiram Bingham's arrival at Machu Picchu. Hiram Bingham is famous for being the first white person to ask a Peruvian where Machu Picchu was. Because of the celebration, Aguas Calientes was even more crowded than usual. Planned celebrations included an elaborate laser light show on the face of the ruins. I'm sure the laser light show was something the Incas had planned too, but never had time to implement. I wanted to take pictures of the sunrise over Machu Picchu, so I set my alarm for four-thirty and crashed.

In the morning of the next day, I dressed and slipped out of our room without waking the others.

My hike on that morning differed from any other I'd made into the ruins.

A long line of people stretched out before me, each wearing a small headlamp to light the path. I joined the line and made my way with them. We were like miners exploring a new network of tunnels.

A half hour into the hike, I realized I, too, should have brought a light. At first I'd been surrounded by people with headlamps. But I was too tired from my Inca Trail hike to keep pace and, as we entered the overhanging jungle, I stumbled over the steps in near total darkness. Then the hiking trail crossed the road that buses took to the ruins, so I selected that path. It was wider and easier to see in the dark.

When the sky began lightening, I returned to the hiking path, only to have Martin come hurdling over me.

"Hi!" he said, with a grin.

"Hi," I replied. "How long ago did you leave the hotel?"

"Oh, about 15 minutes."

I'd been hiking for something like an hour.

"These tourists are driving me nuts," Martin said. "I keep having to leap over them just to get by."

I laughed.

"Well, see you," Martin said, and he bounded up the hill like a wild animal.

When I finally arrived at the gate, I made my way into Machu Picchu, arriving in time to take photos of the spectacular sunrise.

Machu Picchu, just as beautiful as ever, seemed different after the solitude of Choquequirao.

It's true what Heisenberg said, that you cannot observe something without changing it.

Enough people had observed Machu Picchu to make it quite different than Choquequirao. Not in a bad way, but in a recognizable way. Machu Picchu is a shared place: your opinion of it is shaped by the reactions of the thronging tourists who surround you. At Choquequirao, there still exists the possibility of extracting your own unique perspective.

Still, everyone who goes to Machu Picchu is having an adventure, and there excitement fills the air.

I snapped my pictures, took a leisurely walk around the premises, and made my way back to the hotel, where I joined Roberto on the veranda.

At lunch, Roberto and I were sitting at an outdoor table at El Indio Feliz, perhaps the best restaurant in Aguas Calientes. The restaurant was located down a bright yellow alley a few blocks from the Plaza de Armas. I had just lifted up my fork to dig into a plate of chicken and rice served in a pineapple half when Martin came stomping up, agitated.

"What did you think?" Roberto asked, referring to Martin's visit to Machu Picchu.

"Too many people," Martin replied. "I sprinted up to the top of Wayna Picchu and sat there by myself awhile and relaxed. A couple French tourists came along, so I asked them to take my picture. I thanked them and turned around to leave, when they said, 'Aren't you going to stay and enjoy the view?' To which I replied, 'I've been here forty minutes already.' They couldn't believe it; they told me they thought they'd been the first ones to arrive."

Everyone wants to be first; it doesn't matter if you're competing in a race or exploring a national park. Any other day, the French couple would have been first, it was just their misfortune that they'd visited Machu Picchu on the same day as Batman.

As we sat down to a gourmet meal, I realized that during seven years in Perú I'd seen much of the country. Sure, I hadn't visited every amazing site, such as the Nasca lines, but at that moment I felt that I'd covered enough of the major landmarks to have a well-developed sense of the place. More importantly, perhaps, I'd taken the time to learn about the people and the culture, and I had developed a sincere affection for both. Perú is a wonderful nation filled with tremendous beauty, but the true wealth of the country lies within its people. The vast majority of Peruvians are some of the warmest, kindest, most accepting human beings I've ever met, and they are instantly willing to adopt you as one of their own. All rudderless travelers would count themselves thankful if the currents should deposit them in the land of the Incas.

*

We returned to Cusco, then to Lima, and said our goodbyes. Martin insisted that he'd be back the following year to run the trail again, as well as climb some of the bigger, meaner, more jagged-looking peaks visible from the Sacred Valley. Then he was on a plane to the Czech Republic.

Roberto, too, took his leave, flying back to Seattle, Washington, where he lives and trains for the World Cup.

As for me, I'd received a letter from a friend of mine visiting Ecuador as a foreign exchange student. I never need to be invited twice. It was time for a border run anyway, so I purchased a bus ticket and made my way up the coast.

Chapter 42

The Old Fears

My dreamy recollections came to an abrupt halt when once again I found myself in Ecuador, regarding the ominous line of stern-faced mercenaries with AK-47s. The final fragments of my memories dissolved as I took my place among other simple travelers waiting to be judged.

The people on the bus looked through the window, concerned and curious. Nobody was holding up any recording devices. They had too much sense for that.

The mercenaries continued their lethargic process and, in the fragments of eternity that remained, I had no regrets.

I'd had a good run. The air smelled sweet, just as it had atop Wayna Picchu or at the summit of the Yanama Pass.

I'd seen some spectacular sights. I'd made some good friends. I'd helped out a couple people in need, taught a few things to students who might not have learned them otherwise; I'd guided my share of lost travelers on their way. Maybe I could have done more, but at least I'd done something.

Then, like the visage of death himself, the ringleader appeared.

"Documento," he barked.

I gave him my passport.

The fellow furrowed his brow and glared at my little blue book for a few minutes. Finally, he jammed it back in my chest.

"OK," he said, "get back on the bus."

I felt like the wind had been knocked out of me. I stood still for a moment, my whole body numb. I thought it must be a trick. At any moment, the mercenaries would unsling their rifles and start shooting us while cackling peals of cruel laughter.

The ringleader noticed my hesitation and looked at me. "What's the matter?"

"I can go?"

"Yeah," he said, "this is a checkpoint. What did you think it was?"

I didn't answer.

The soldier took the passport of the next person in line. As he looked at it, he muttered, "Typical American, freaking out about nothing."

Feeling numb, I made my way back onto the bus and into my semi-comfortable seat, from which I watched the proceedings through the smeary window. After a little while, the bus began to pull away. A couple of the mercenaries reached up their hands in friendly waves.

I waved back.

"Typical American," I said, repeating the soldier's comment, "freaking out about nothing." I thought about his words for a moment. Then I began to laugh.

Hadn't I learned anything?

The bus rattled. The trees turned into a green mist. A moment of silence ensued. I didn't feel inclined to be too hard on myself. We are all works in progress. The lessons I had picked up throughout the years were not of the type to be adopted and then forgotten. No, these lessons required constant reminding, and still it was possible to fall back into old habits of thought.

Travel helps separate what is real from what is not.

Travel is education without agenda, and the person who completes a journey can depend on being improved over the one who set out.

The world changes so fast that knowledge becomes outdated, and much of what is generally believed gradually ceases to be true. New explorations of old places yield ever new discoveries. Danger becomes safety and safety becomes danger. At the beginning there is no way of accurately discerning the prudent path from the reckless one. We can only aspire to distil truth from perception and let reason prevail.

Made in the USA
San Bernardino, CA
18 September 2017